P9-DFF-120

Meet Yourself in the Parables

Warren W. Wiersbe

This book is designed for your personal
reading pleasure and profit. It is also
designed for group study. A leader's guide
with helps and hints for teachers and
visual aids (Victor Multiuse Transparency
Masters) is available from your local book-
store or from the publisher.

VICTOR BOOKS

a division of SP Publications, Inc.
WHEATON. ILLINOIS 60187

Offices also in Fullerton, California • Whitby, Ontario, Canada • Amersham-on-the-Hill, Bucks, England

Fifth printing, 1981

Scripture quotations in this book are from the
Authorized (King James) Version, unless otherwise
noted. Other quotations are from the *New American
Standard Bible* (NASB), ©1960, 1962, 1963, 1968,
1971, 1973 by The Lockman Foundation, La Habra,
California; and *The New Testament in Modern
English* (PH), ©1958 by J. B. Phillips, The Macmil-
lan Company.

Recommended Dewey Decimal Number: 226.8
Suggested Subject Headings: PARABLES; JESUS CHRIST—PARABLES

Library of Congress Catalog Card Number: 79-64845
ISBN: 0–88207–877–1

©1979 by SP Publications, Inc. All rights reserved
Printed in the United States of America

VICTOR BOOKS
A division of SP Publications, Inc.
P.O. Box 1825 • Wheaton, Illinois 61087

Dedicated to my friend
Tedd Seelye:
a gifted communicator
a stimulating conversationalist
a co-laborer in sharing the Word

Contents

Preface

In my ministry, I have always been partial to the parables. No matter how many times I have studied them, I always discover something new, and I always see myself in a new light. I have preached and taught some of the parables dozens of times, and yet they have never grown old.

But let me warn you: studying the parables is like exposing yourself to a laser beam! It is a dangerous thing to approach our Lord's parables with a careless attitude. In these stories, Jesus deals with subjects that no Christian can afford to treat lightly: salvation, forgiveness of others, love for minority groups, the right and wrong use of money, prayer, motives for service, and many more.

In these studies, I have tried to shed some new light on familiar truths. The parables are not bedtime stories to put us to sleep, but bugle calls to wake us up! So, if you find yourself jolted by some lesson that is taught, give thanks to God and immediately apply that lesson to your life.

I have always met myself in the parables, and I suspect you will meet yourself as well. But don't be afraid! It will do us both good!

Warren W. Wiersbe

Matthew 13:10–17, 34–35, 51–52

[10]And the disciples came, and said unto Him, "Why speakest thou unto them in parables?" [11]He answered and said unto them, "Because it is given unto you to know the mysteries of the kingdom of heaven, but to them it is not given. [12]For whosoever hath, to him shall be given, and he shall have more abundance: but whosoever hath not, from him shall be taken away even that he hath. [13]Therefore speak I to them in parables: because they seeing see not; and hearing they hear not, neither do they understand. [14]And in them is fulfilled the prophecy of Esaias, which saith, 'By hearing ye shall hear, and shall not understand; and seeing ye shall see, and shall not perceive: [15]For this people's heart is waxed gross, and their ears are dull of hearing, and their eyes they have closed; lest at any time they should see with their eyes, and hear with their ears, and should understand with their heart, and should be converted, and I should heal them.' [16]But blessed are your eyes, for they see: and your ears, for they hear. [17]For verily I say unto you, that many prophets and righteous men have desired to see those things which ye see, and have not seen them; and to hear those things which ye hear, and have not heard them." [34]All these things spake Jesus unto the multitude in parables; and without a parable spake He not unto them: [35]That it might be fulfilled which was spoken by the prophet, saying, "I will open My mouth in parables; I will utter things which have been kept secret from the foundation of the world." [51]Jesus saith unto them, "Have ye understood all these things?" They said unto Him, "Yea, Lord." [52]Then said He unto them, "Therefore every scribe which is instructed unto the kingdom of heaven is like unto a man that is an householder, which bringeth forth out of his treasure things new and old."

1

But Why Parables?
The Parable of the Householder

Even His disciples were surprised on that day in Capernaum, by the Sea of Galilee, when Jesus spoke the series of parables recorded in Matthew 13. They learned that there is more to parabolic teaching than just telling a story.

Our English word "parable" is a transliteration of the Greek *parabole* (pronounced para-bow-LAY) which simply means "to place beside, to cast alongside." A parable, then, is a story that places one thing beside another for the purpose of teaching. It puts the known next to the unknown so that we may learn. When Jesus said, "The kingdom of heaven is like . . . ," He was using comparison or contrast to teach a spiritual lesson.

Some parables are long and detailed, such as the parable of the sower (Matt. 13:3–9), while others are quite brief, such as the parable of the householder (Matt. 13:52). The word "parable" is used 48 times in the first three Gospels, twice in Hebrews (9:9 and 11:19), and nowhere else in the New Testament. The word translated "parable" in the Authorized Version of John 10:6 is not *parabole*, but *paroimia*, which is better translated "figure of speech" or "proverb."

The familiar definition of a parable as "an earthly

story with a heavenly meaning" does not say it all, but
it says enough, and it reminds us that there is a unity
between the visible world of nature and the invisible
world of the spiritual. God has revealed truth to us in
creation as well as in the Bible. The fact that Jesus
could use a seed to explain the Word of God, or a feast
to explain salvation, is evidence that all truth comes
from God and all truth is a unity. The better we know
the book of nature, the better we will know the Word
of God, if we are yielded to Christ and open to His
teaching.

Why Did Jesus Teach in Parables?

Our Lord did not invent the parable. You will find
parables in the Old Testament (2 Samuel 12:1–4, for
example), and the Jewish rabbis used them often.
Jesus, however, was certainly the greatest exponent
of parabolic teaching.

When His disciples asked Him the reason for His
teaching in parables, the Lord replied by quoting a
prophecy found in Isaiah 6:9–10. This is one of the
most important prophecies in the Old Testament, and
it is quoted five times in the New Testament (Matt.
13:14–15; Mark 4:12; Luke 8:10; John 12:39–40; Acts
28:26–27). This prophecy refers to the spiritual
deterioration of the people of Israel. They would hear
God's Word but not understand it, and they would
see God's power at work, but not perceive what He
was doing. Their dull hearts would make them
spiritually blind and deaf, and the result would be
judgment.

Interpreters face a problem with these verses.
When Matthew quoted our Lord's answer, he had
Him say, "Therefore speak I to them in parables:
because they seeing see not" (v. 13, italics mine). But
Mark and Luke used the word *that* and not the word

because (see Mark 4:11–12 and Luke 8:10). Mark and Luke stated that Jesus used parables *so that* people might not see and hear, and so on. Does this mean that Jesus told parables so that His listeners would be condemned? This seems contrary to the character and ministry of our Lord.

It seems to me that *both* are true. By using parables, our Lord was seeking to interest and awaken those whose spiritual senses were growing dull. The Jewish people in general, and their religious leaders in particular, were involved in a process that was deadening their spiritual perceptions. The tense of the Greek verb in Matthew 13:14 indicates this: "For in them is being fulfilled . . ." The process was not completed, and the Lord wanted to arrest it. By telling stories with hidden meanings, He was arousing their interest and giving them opportunity to be saved.

But the other aspect of this prophecy is also true: the same message that awakens one will harden another. These parables both revealed and concealed. The careless and indifferent, those with no spiritual hunger for truth and salvation, would not understand His teaching. It is not that His Word would harden their hearts so much as their hearts were hardened against His Word. The same sun that melts the ice also hardens the clay. By using parables, the Lord was revealing His patience and mercy, but at the same time He revealed their sad spiritual condition. The parables were the words of a master Teacher, but they were also the sentences of a holy Judge.

It would be wise for us to include Mark 4:21–25 and Luke 8:16–18 in this study, for many students of Scripture believe that Jesus spoke these words in conjunction with the parables of Matthew 13. Here is Mark's record:

And He said unto them, "Is a candle brought to be put under a bushel, or under a bed? and not to be set on a candlestick? [22]For there is nothing hid, which shall not be manifested; neither was any thing kept secret, but that it should come abroad. [23]If any man have ears to hear, let him hear." [24]And He said unto them, "Take heed what ye hear: with what measure ye mete, it shall be measured to you: and unto you that hear shall more be given. [25]For he that hath, to him shall be given: and he that hath not, from him shall be taken even that which he hath."

Jesus seems to be teaching here that He has hidden the truth in parables, not to conceal it, but to reveal it. The man who has faith will learn the truth and receive more while the man who lacks faith will lose even what he thinks he has. In other words, when we hear the Word of God, we are not participating in a static event, but in a dynamic experience. We are either the better or the worse for having heard God's Word.

Jesus used parables to hide the truth so that He might reveal the truth. A parable would excite the concerned and stimulate them to learn more. But it would also blind the careless and, because of their condition of heart, hasten their judgment.

A second reason for the use of parables is given in Matthew 13:34–35: it was the fulfillment of the prophecy written in Psalm 78:2. "I will open my mouth in a parable: I will utter dark sayings of old." The prophet who wrote these words was Asaph, the seer (2 Chron. 29:30). Originally, the statement referred to his own explanation of the spiritual meaning of Israel's history, which he covers in his psalm. But the long-range meaning relates to Christ. In His parables, Jesus opened to us the "mysteries" (hidden secrets understood only by divine revelation). One of Matthew's purposes in writing his Gospel was to show how Jesus Christ, in His life and teaching, fulfilled the Old Testament Scriptures. "That it might be fulfilled" is one of his key statements (see 1:22; 2:15, 17, 23; 4:14).

We must not criticize Christ because His parables brought judgment to some and salvation to others. This "gaining and losing" is a law of life. If we use what we have, we receive more; if we neglect to use it, we lose it. While this does not apply in every area of life, it is generally true. His disciples (except for Judas) possessed saving faith, and therefore received more through an understanding of the parables. But the unbelievers, in opposing the truth, would lose and their hearts would become harder.

Why Study the Parables?

The most obvious reason for studying the parables is that they are part of the Word of God and we have been commanded to live on "every word" (Matt. 4:4). Also, at least one-third of Christ's recorded teaching is found in parables. To ignore these stories is to rob ourselves of much that He wants us to learn.

But something else is true. The parables were "born out of life," and therefore have a way of touching us in those areas where life is the most meaningful and significant. Even though we may not live in a rural environment, learning about seeds and soil is important to us. How many times have we said, or heard, "Let me *plant* this idea in your mind"?

Many parables were given because of some opposition or problem. The Pharisees criticized Jesus for eating with sinners, so He told about a lost sheep, a lost coin, and a lost son. The disciples thought they were very successful because of the big crowds, so He told the story about the sower who saw three-fourths of his seed produce nothing. He was accused of being in league with the devil, so He told about the strong man guarding his castle. These stories deal with the realities and the essentials of life and for this reason, they are important to us.

The parables are both mirrors and windows. As mirrors, they help us see ourselves. They reveal our lives as they really are. As windows, they help us see life and God. You may not have an easy time identifying with some truth in Romans 7 or Ephesians 2, but you probably have little difficulty seeing yourself in one of the parables.

How Should We Study the Parables?

Because you find different kinds of literature in the Bible, it is important to know how to deal with each kind. You do not approach the poetry of the Psalms in the same way that you approach the narratives of Bible history or the doctrinal discussions of the epistles. It is a basic rule of Bible study that we examine each passage of Scripture in the light of its literary classification.

With this in mind, consider these principles for interpreting the parables.

1. Study each parable in its context. This is true of any portion of Scripture, but it is especially true of the parables. Ignore the context and you can make a parable teach almost anything. For example, the parable of the good Samaritan has suffered at the hands of "spiritualizers" who have forgotten the context. They interpret Jerusalem as the city of God, representing heaven. Jericho is a condemned city, so it represents hell. The road from Jerusalem to Jericho goes *down,* and so does the road to hell. Each person is a pilgrim on the Jericho Road and has been robbed by Satan and left half-dead (alive physically, dead spiritually). Religion cannot save him—only Christ (the Good Samaritan) can. The oil represents the Holy Spirit and the wine Christ's shed blood. The inn is the church and the two pence stand for the two ordinances. The Samaritan promised to come again, and Jesus will come again.

Many of these things are true, and are taught in the Bible; but they are not *expressly* taught in the parable of the Good Samaritan. The context is the lawyer's evasive question, "And who is my neighbor?" While there is certainly a salvation message in this parable, the fundamental lesson is that of being a neighbor to those in need.

2. Look for the main truth the parable teaches. This does not mean there are no secondary lessons, but even these must be related to the main message of the parable. The main message of the parable of the prodigal son is that God receives and forgives sinners. You can discover in this rich parable many spiritual truths, but all of them relate in some way to that primary lesson.

3. Don't try to make the parable "walk on all fours." Some of the parables are quite detailed, such as the sower and the tares, while others have very little detail. It is not necessary to make everything mean something unless the context warrants it. Jesus explained the parable of the sower in detail, and likewise the parable of the tares, so there is no problem. But the example of spiritualizing the parable of the good Samaritan shows what can happen if a meaning is attached to every detail.

In connection with this principle, the symbols used in different parables do not always represent the same thing. In the parable of the sower, the seed represents the Word of God and soil represents the human heart. But in the parable of the tares, the seed represents the children of the kingdom, while the field is the world.

4. *The parables were given to illustrate doctrine, not to declare it*. In other words, don't try to build a case for some doctrine *only* on the basis of a parable. The parables are the windows in the house, not the foundation stones. It would be dangerous to build a doctrine of salvation by good works on the parable of the sheep and goats (Matt. 25:31ff). To do so would be to ignore the prophetic context of the parable, and the resulting "doctrine" would contradict the clear teaching of other Scriptures.

5. *Ask God for spiritual perception*. This is necessary for all Bible study, but it is especially important in dealing with the parables. The disciples came to Jesus and asked Him for understanding, and you and I must do likewise. He will give us the wisdom that we need (see James 1:5).

How Shall We Best Use the Parables?

The parable of the householder explains how to best use the parables (Matt 13:52). Our Lord asked His disciples if they understood *all* that He had taught them, and they responded, "Yes." (Their answer has always amazed me!) Understanding always means responsibility. The disciples were privileged to understand hidden truths, and therefore they had a great responsibility to put these truths into practice. "For unto whomsoever much is given, of him shall be much required" (Luke 12:48).

Jesus said, "Therefore every scribe who has become a disciple of heaven is like a head of a household, who brings forth out of his treasure things new and old" (Matt. 13:52, NASB). In this statement (which is a brief parable), He pointed out three responsibilities that we have toward God's truth.

1. The responsibility of learning the truth. A scribe's work was to examine the Law and discover its teachings. It is important to remember that the scribes began as a very noble group. They devoted themselves to the protection and preservation of the Law. But sad to say, the scribes degenerated into an unspiritual clique and were more interested in protecting dead tradition than teaching living truth. Jesus accused them of putting the people under spiritual bondage, not liberty (Luke 11:46–52). They so revered the past that they ignored God's lessons in the present. Instead of opening doors for sinners to be saved, they closed them. They became blind leaders of the blind. Why? Because they had not become disciples.

2. The responsibility of living the truth. Every scribe must become a disciple, a person who follows the Lord and puts His truth into practice. We *learn* the *truth* to live the truth. The truth becomes alive to us when we live it, and in the process we learn more truth! A desperate need exists today for a balance between theory and practice, learning and living, the schoolroom and the marketplace. Jesus taught His disciples by precept *and by practice.* There was a balance between objective truth and subjective experience. It is not enough to be hearers of the Word— we must be *doers* if we are going to grow and glorify God.

3. The responsibility of sharing the truth. Each of us has a treasury within that contains the spiritual currency we have accumulated from our learning and living. This treasure of spiritual truth must be shared. Money that is not invested is wasted because it accomplishes nothing useful. In the same way, we must share the old and the new. The "old" is what we have learned as scribes; the "new" is what we learn as disciples, practicing the truth. *It is those who obey God's Word who learn the most of God's Word and have the most to share*. We cannot do without the old, for out of the old comes the new. There are always new applications of old truths, new insights into old principles, and new understandings of old relationships.

I think Ezra, the first scribe, exemplified this kind of balanced life. It was said of this man of God: "For Ezra had prepared his heart to seek the law of the Lord [the scribe-learning], and to do it [the disciple-living], and to teach in Israel statutes and judgments [the householder-sharing]" (Ezra 7:10). What a good example to follow!

Have You Met Yourself in This Parable?

1. Do you find yourself excited or bored by a study of the parables?

2. Perhaps you find yourself *frightened*? Are you afraid of what you may learn about yourself?

3. Do you sincerely strive for spiritual understanding? (See Proverbs 2:1–6.)

4. Are you willing to practice what the parables teach you? Are you a disciple as well as a scribe?

5. How full is your spiritual treasury? Are you dispensing only the "old" because you have not acquired anything "new"?

6. Do you keep your spiritual wealth to yourself?

Matthew 13:1–9, 18–23

[1]The same day went Jesus out of the house, and sat by the sea side.
[2]And great multitudes were gathered together unto Him, so that
He went into a ship, and sat; and the whole multitude stood on the
shore. [3]And He spake many things unto them in parables, saying,
"Behold, a sower went forth to sow; [4]And when he sowed, some
seeds fell by the way side, and the fowls came and devoured them
up: [5]some fell upon stony places, where they had not much earth:
and forthwith they sprung up, because they had no deepness of
earth: [6]and when the sun was up, they were scorched; and because
they had no root, they withered away. [7]And some fell among
thorns; and the thorns sprung up, and choked them: [8]but other fell
into good ground, and brought forth fruit, some an hundredfold,
some sixtyfold, some thirtyfold. [9]Who hath ears to hear, let him
hear. [18]Hear ye therefore the parable of the sower. [19]When any one
heareth the word of the kingdom, and understandeth it not, then
cometh the wicked one, and catcheth away that which was sown in
his heart. This is he which received seed by the way side. [20]But he
that received the seed in stony places, the same is he that heareth
the word, and anon with joy receiveth it; [21]yet hath he not root in
himself, but dureth for a while: for when tribulation or persecution
ariseth because of the word, by and by he is offended. [22]He also
that received seed among the thorns is he that heareth the word;
and the care of this world, and the deceitfulness of riches, choke
the word, and he becometh unfruitful. [23]But he that received seed
into the good ground is he that heareth the word, and understandeth it; which also beareth fruit, and bringeth forth, some an
hundredfold, some sixty, some thirty."

2

The Way to a Man's Heart Is Through His Ears
The Parable of the Sower

Did you ever wonder what happens to all the preaching and teaching that goes on in this world? Christians speak and write millions of words daily, and yet so little seems to come from it. Has God's Word lost its power? Is there something wrong with the way we share the Word?

The parable of the sower helps to answer these and other questions about the ministry of the Word. If you understand this parable, you will know better how to use the Bible and how to share it with others. You will also not be discouraged by seeming failure or falsely encouraged by shallow success. This is a basic parable. "Know ye not this parable?" Jesus asked His disciples. "And how then will ye know all parables?" (Mark 4:13)

Three basic symbols are important in the parable of the sower.

The Seed Is the Word of God

Why did Jesus compare God's Word to seed? To begin with, *seed has life in it*. God's Word is a living Word (1 Peter 1:23). The books that men write are dead, no matter how helpful or interesting they may be. They cannot impart life as the Word of God can. If you want to grow a living plant, you must begin with a living seed.

Like a seed, God's Word may seem small and insignificant, but it is powerful. Have you ever seen a sidewalk cracked and broken because of a seed? When placed next to the learned books of this world, the Bible may not look any different, but it is powerful, living, and active (Heb. 4:12).

Like a seed, God's Word *produces fruit* and that fruit has in it the seed for more fruit. Tremendous potential lies in a seed. When the Word of God gets into a human heart and germinates and grows, spiritual fruit is eventually seen in that life. God's Word can produce different kinds of spiritual fruit in our lives:

- winning souls to Christ—Romans 1:13
- practical holiness—Romans 6:22
- sharing material things—Romans 15:27
- Christian character—Galatians 5:22–23
- good works—Colossians 1:10
- praise and witness—Hebrews 13:15

The Word, like seed, must be planted to do any good. It must be cultivated, nurtured, and protected. Jesus explained in this parable that it is not enough for the believer to listen to the Word. He must *hear* it, receive it into his heart, and let it take root and grow. Seven times in this parable, and 19 times in Matthew 13, Jesus used the word *hear*. He was not talking only about the physical act of listening to words and sounds. He was talking about listening with the inner ear and receiving God's Word deep into the heart.

The Sower Is One Who Shares the Word

Originally, the sower who shared the Word was Jesus Christ. He should have come as a reaper, but there was no harvest. The Jewish nation had rejected God's

Word and turned to the teaching and traditions of men. The scribes and Pharisees had so encrusted the seed of the Word with their traditions that Jesus had to break these traditions to recover the lost seed. Then He had to break the husk of the seed (the mere letter of the Word) to reveal the living kernel within. We need that same process repeated today.

It takes faith for a person to sow seed. Our Lord called 12 men together and taught them the truths of the Word of God. The future of God's work in the world depended on how their hearts responded to the Word. They, with the exception of Judas, taught the truth to others (2 Tim. 2:2), and because of their faithfulness you and I have the Word today.

Anyone who shares God's Word today is a sower. Seed may be a polished sermon, a simple witness to a friend, a sentence in a letter, or even a song—but if it contains the Word, it is seed being sown. It is important not to try to improve on God's spiritual seed. "You shall not sow your field with two kinds of seed" (Lev. 19:19) was a practical admonition to Israel that carries a deeper spiritual lesson to us today. Do not sow the Word of God *plus* man's philosophies, man's theories, man's traditions. Just sow the pure Word of God. A good farmer washes his seed before he sows it. A good spiritual farmer makes sure he does not mix God's Word with anything defiling.

A sower must have *personal concern*. "They that sow in tears shall reap in joy. He that goeth forth and weepeth, bearing precious seed, shall doubtless come again with rejoicing, bringing his sheaves with him" (Ps. 126:5–6). He must water the seed with his tears if he expects to see a harvest.

A principle of *partnership* must operate if there is to be a harvest. "I have planted, Apollos watered; but God gave the increase" (1 Cor. 3:6). Jesus emphasized this principle when He talked about the harvest in Samaria: "Other men labored, and ye are entered into their labors" (read John 4:35–38). There must be no competition in the harvest: "We are God's fellow-workers" (1 Cor. 3:9, NASB).

A pastor once invited an evangelist to hold a campaign in his church. The people were prepared for him and God blessed in a remarkable way. But the pastor became envious of the evangelist and told several members that he would never invite him back again. Instead of rejoicing that the seed he had planted in the previous months was bearing fruit, the pastor became bitter and critical. The Bible makes it clear that *God gives the increase*, not man, and the sower and reaper should rejoice together because they are rewarded together.

Patience is needed to sow. "Behold, the farmer waits for the precious produce of the soil, being patient about it, until it gets the early and late rains" (James 5:7, NASB). He dare not harvest too soon: "First the blade, then the ear, after that the full corn in the ear" (Mark 4:28).

How unfortunate it is that some believers are sowing everything else but the Word of God! Some are sowing to their flesh (Gal. 6:7–8) and will reap a tragic harvest of sin. Others are sowing discord (Prov. 6:19). You and I have been called to sow the truth of God's Word, and we must be faithful to the Lord of the harvest.

The Soil Represents the Human Heart

Man is made from the earth, so it is no surprise that Christ compared the human heart to soil. To begin with, *soil has great potential*. A plot of ground can become a jungle or a garden. If you have ever visited Victoria, British Columbia, you may have seen the famous Butchart Gardens. My family and I walked through these beautiful gardens one June day, and were amazed at what we saw. And to think that the gardens were once an abandoned gravel pit!

Perhaps you have heard about the man who took an ugly vacant lot and turned it into a lovely garden. A passerby said to him, "God has certainly made a beautiful garden here." To which the gardener replied, "You should have seen this lot when God had it by Himself!" The point is well-taken. God uses human instruments to get the best out of the soil. Left to itself, a heart will run riot with sin. But if a heart responds to the ministry of the Word, there can be fruit and beauty.

Since God's Word is seed, and our hearts are soil, our hearts can respond to God's Word. They are made for each other. This does not mean that the human heart is *naturally* spiritual (see 1 Cor. 2:14), but it does mean that when the seed and the soil get together there can be germination, and there can be fruit.

This story is usually called "the parable of the sower" or "the parable of the seed," but the emphasis is really on *the soils*. Jesus explains that there are four kinds of hearts in this world, and He identifies them according to the way they respond to the seed of God's Word.

1. The hard heart (Matt. 13:19). Keep in mind that little footpaths run through the fields in Palestine, so it would not be unusual for some of the seed to fall on hard soil. Such soil represents the person who does not understand the Word of God. He hears but does not comprehend. The seed lies on the surface of the soil and never sinks in. Satan sees it and, like a bird, swoops down and snatches it away. It is gone!

Understanding must precede spiritual life. To plant

seed means the Word is understood and responded to. For someone to give mental assent to a series of religious statements is not the same as having a spiritual understanding of the truth.

In this illustration, the fault did not lie with the seed, the problem was with the soil. It was too hard. But can a hard heart be changed? Yes, it can be plowed up and prepared for the seed. The prophet Hosea advised, "Break up your fallow ground, for it is time to seek the Lord" (Hosea 10:12).

2. *The shallow heart (Matt. 13:20–21)*. The soil in Palestine lies on a thick layer of limestone. Where the soil is thin, the roots of a germinating seed cannot go very far. As a result, the shoot springs up quickly but there is no root system to sustain the plant. No roots mean no water. When the sun comes up, the shoot is scorched and dies.

This represents an emotional hearer who hears the Word but does not really receive it so that it is rooted in his heart. His response is purely emotional, shallow, and temporary. Jesus was not saying that the man (or woman) was saved and then lost his or her salvation. He was saying that the person never had salvation to begin with! It was a shallow, emotional experience that was only on the surface.

Sun is good for a plant but in this case the sun destroyed the plant. In the parable, the sun represents persecution. *Persecution is good for God's child*. It tests a person's faith, proves the reality of his profession, and helps him grow. But all of this is true *if* a person is truly born again and has spiritual roots. Just as the sun helps the plant to draw up water and nourishment from the soil, so suffering and persecution help the true believer trust the Lord and draw on His great resources. *But there must be roots*.

The problem with a hard heart was lack of understanding, and the problem with the shallow heart was lack of depth. This brings us to the third kind of soil and heart.

3. *The crowded heart (Matt. 13:22).* It is not enough for a gardener to love flowers and fruits. He must also hate weeds. The soil described in verse 22 was not clean. It had in it seeds for noxious plants. The sower could not see these foreign seeds, of course, but they were there. *Weeds grow naturally.* No farmer has to plant weeds—they come whether he wants them or not.

The weeds represent those influences from the world that choke the seed and keep it from bearing fruit. Jesus identified these weeds as "the care of this world, and the deceitfulness of riches" (v. 22). In theological terms, the person with this heart never really repented and turned from his sins. He received the Word, but the soil was infested with other seeds and when they germinated the weeds crowded out the good plants. The earth did not produce thorns until sin entered the world (see Gen. 3:17-19). The thorns in this section of the parable represent that which is sinful.

The Bible does not condemn wealth as such, but it does warn that wealth can be a cause of sin and a hindrance to spiritual growth. Riches are deceitful because they promise much more than they can produce. Their value is always changing and they are no guarantee of security. Yet most people in the world devote themselves to the pursuit of riches and ignore the true wealth found in Jesus Christ.

Our Lord knew that many of the people in that crowd on the shore were not receiving His Word into their hearts. Some were thinking about food, clothing, and how to pay their bills. Others were worrying about problems in their lives. These "weeds" were crowding out the good seed and keeping it from bearing fruit.

It is important to note that none of these first three hearts underwent salvation. The proof of salvation is not listening to the Word, or having a quick emotional response to the Word, or even cultivating the Word so that it grows in a life. The proof of salvation is *fruit*, for as Christ said, "Ye shall know them by their fruits" (Matt. 7:16).

4. The fruitful heart (13:23). The fact that Jesus called this heart "good ground" does not mean He was saying people basically have good hearts. The heart of man is basically sinful, and, apart from the working of God's grace, it could never receive God's Word and produce fruit for God's glory. This heart is good in contrast to the other three hearts. It receives the Word (unlike the shallow heart), understands the Word (unlike the hard heart), and holds fast what it receives (unlike the crowded heart). If you combine the descriptions in Matthew 13:23, Mark 4:20, and Luke 8:15, you discover all of these characteristics, and they lead to fruitfulness.

An illustration of these four kinds of hearts is given in John 4, where our Lord dealt with the sinful Samaritan woman. Notice the changes in her heart as the result of His counseling.

Her heart was hard at first, and John explained the reason for her hardness: "for the Jews have no dealings with the Samaritans" (John 4:9). The woman was surprised that a Jewish man, and a rabbi at that, would talk with her in public. She had no understanding of her need or what Jesus had to offer her.

Her hard heart became a shallow heart. The Lord offered her living water, and she immediately replied, "Sir, give me this water, that I thirst not, neither come hither to draw" (John 4:15). This was an emotional response that had no depth to it. The Lord knew this, so He immediately began to plow up her heart: "Go, call thy husband!" This was touching the most sensitive part of her life, for she had been living a wicked life.

What happened next? She developed a crowded heart—she began to argue about religion. The old weeds of prejudice and worldliness began to grow. Jesus refused to get into an argument over whether Jerusalem or Samaria was the place to worship. Her greatest need was to worship God in Spirit and in truth. At that point, the good seed that had been planted in her heart years ago began to grow. She said, "I know that Messiah is coming . . . when that One comes, He will declare all things to us" (John 4:25, NASB). Jesus then revealed who He was, she believed, and immediately she began to bear fruit.

Many of us would not have been as patient as Jesus was when He dealt with her. When she said, "Give me this water" we would have instantly prayed with her and assured her she was saved! But Jesus knew better. He knew that her response was a shallow one that could not last. He kept dealing with her until the soil of her heart was ready to respond to the offer of salvation.

Those of us who have experienced salvation need to learn from this parable the importance of cultivating our own hearts and planting the Word. Unless we spend time planting the Word (understanding it) and cultivating it (meditating and praying), we cannot be fruitful Christians. We must be certain that our soil is free from weeds, plowed up, and ready to receive God's Word.

If a Christian neglects the cultivation of his heart, the soil will start to deteriorate. The good soil will soon become crowded soil. The weeds will sap the strength from the soil, and it will become shallow. Then it will become hard. The Epistle to the Hebrews was written to warn Christians not to become hard hearted as they hear the Word of God (see Hebrews 4:7–16).

The secret of a fruitful heart is a hearing ear. Each of the first three Gospels gives a warning at the end of the section that records the parable of the sower. Matthew wrote, "He who has ears, let him hear" (13:9, NASB). In other words, give attention to the Word of God. Take advantage of every opportunity to receive the good seed into your heart.

Mark cautioned, "Take care what you listen to" (4:24, NASB). Whatever you hear enters into your mind and heart. It is seed that is planted, and will bear fruit. If you plant weeds, you will reap a sad harvest of sin. "Be not deceived; God is not mocked: for whatsoever a man soweth, that shall he also reap" (Gal. 6:7). This explains why a Christian should be careful in what he reads, the kind of entertainment he watches, the kind of conversation and music he listens to.

Luke admonished, "Take care how you listen" (8:18, NASB). It is a sad fact that most people do not know how to hear. We are a society of spectators—we know how to watch but not how to hear and listen. Since "faith cometh by hearing, and hearing by the Word of God" (Rom. 10:17), it is important that we learn how to hear God's Word. Church members like to blame dull teachers and preachers for their lack of spiritual growth, but perhaps the problem is *dull hearers*. (See Hebrews 5:11–14.)

As Christians, we must take care of our spiritual sense of hearing. We must beware of only wanting to hear new and sensational things (2 Tim. 4:3) which may turn us away from God's truth (2 Tim. 4:4), or even stop up our ears so that we refuse to listen to God's voice (Acts 7:57). We need the attitude young Samuel had when he said, "Speak Lord, for Thy servant heareth" (1 Sam. 3:10). Remember the admonitions: "Take heed *that* you hear, take heed *what* you hear, and take heed *how* you hear!"

Have You Met Yourself in This Parable?

1. What is your attitude toward the Word of God?
2. What is the condition of the soil of your heart?
3. What fruit has come from your life recently?
4. Are you sowing the Word patiently, seeking to use discernment and wisdom?
5. Are you helping others bear fruit?

Luke 5:27–39

²⁷And after these things He went forth, and saw a publican, named Levi, sitting at the receipt of custom: and He said unto him, "Follow Me." ²⁸And he left all, rose up, and followed Him. ²⁹And Levi made him a great feast in his own house: and there was a great company of publicans and of others that sat down with them. ³⁰But their scribes and Pharisees murmured against His disciples, saying, "Why do ye eat and drink with publicans and sinners?" ³¹And Jesus answering said unto them, "They that are whole need not a physician; but they that are sick. ³²I came not to call the righteous, but sinners to repentance." ³³And they said unto Him, "Why do the disciples of John fast often, and make prayers, and likewise the disciples of the Pharisees; but Thine eat and drink?" ³⁴And He said unto them, "Can ye make the children of the bridechamber fast, while the bridegroom is with them? ³⁵But the days will come, when the bridegroom shall be taken away from them, and then shall they fast in those days." ³⁶And He spake also a parable unto them; "No man putteth a piece of a new garment upon an old; if otherwise, then both the new maketh a rent, and the piece that was taken out of the new agreeth not with the old. ³⁷And no man putteth new wine into old bottles; else the new wine will burst the bottles, and be spilled, and the bottles shall perish. ³⁸But new wine must be put into new bottles; and both are preserved. ³⁹No man also having drunk old wine straightway desireth new: for he saith, 'The old is better.' "

3
Something Old, Something New
The Parable of the Cloth and Wineskins

The news spread through Capernaum as only news can spread in a middle eastern city.

"Levi, the son of Alpheus, has been converted! He is leaving his position as tax collector to follow Jesus of Nazareth. He even has a new name—Matthew. And he is giving a great feast to celebrate his new life!"

There were many publicans and sinners (Jews who did not follow the Law) at the feast, and this gave Christ's enemies opportunity to criticize Him.

"Why do You eat and drink with publicans and sinners?" they asked Him. "You claim to be a teacher from God, and yet You eat bread with those who have disobeyed God!"

Then the disciples of John the Baptist showed up with a question: "Why do we and the Pharisees fast, but you and Your disciples are feasting?" (I wonder if they had been urged to get into the discussion by the Pharisees?)

These two questions, and the general misunderstanding among the people, led Jesus to use three illustrations to explain why He had come and what it was He wanted to accomplish. Even today, Jesus and His ministry are misunderstood. One preacher calls Him an Example, another says He is a Teacher, and a third is certain that He is a Rebel who came to overthrow the system. The Jews wanted Him to be a militant conquerer, the Pharisees wanted Him to be a religious conformist, and today He is looked upon as the "gentle Carpenter" and the "first Christian."

He Is a Physician Who Came for Sinners (5:27–32)

The Pharisees were offended because Jesus was eating with people who did not belong to the upper crust of Capernaum—people who were known to be sinners of one kind or another. You must remember that sharing a meal meant much more in the Middle East than it does in our Western culture. To eat bread was to form a covenant, to bind yourselves as friends and allies. This is one reason why Jesus instituted a meal as a church ordinance; it reminds us that we belong to Him and to each other.

When the Pharisees looked at the guests, they saw sinners and wanted nothing to do with them. It is interesting that the Pharisees always *repelled* sinners, while Jesus *attracted* them. "Then drew near unto Him [Jesus] all the publicans and sinners for to hear Him. And the Pharisees and scribes murmured, saying, 'This man receiveth sinners and eateth with them' " (Luke 15:1–2). Of course, the Pharisees had no message of hope for lost sinners. It was Jesus who came "to seek and to save that which was lost" (Luke 19:10).

But Jesus did not look at these people and see hopeless outcasts or criminals who needed a judge. He saw people who were desperately sick and needed a physician. Many pictures of sin are given in the Bible: defilement (Ps. 51:1–2), darkness (John 3:17–19), bondage (Ps. 107:10–14), and even death (Eph. 2:1; Rom. 6:23). But *disease* is frequently used to illustrate sin. The prophet Isaiah used disease to picture Israel's sins: "the whole head is sick, and the whole heart faint. From the sole of the foot even unto the head there is no soundness in it. But wounds, and bruises, and putrifying sores; they have not been closed, neither bound up, neither mollified with ointment" (Isa. 1:5–6). Jeremiah wrote, "The heart is more deceitful than all else and is desperately sick" (17:9, NASB).

Using sickness as a picture of sin, its origin can be traced to an invasion of germs. Sin enters our lives secretly and infects us. There is a period of decline, and then a sudden failure. Perhaps the person collapses! He experiences pain and he may be infectious to others. If the germs are not destroyed, they will destroy him. Paul wrote, "the wages of sin is death" (Rom. 6:23).

Some sicknesses are obvious. You can look at the person and know he is ill. But some are not so obvious. I recall visiting a beautiful little girl in a hospital, admiring her healthy-looking features, and then discovering she was dying of leukemia. The publicans and sinners were spiritually sick, and they knew it. But the Pharisees were also spiritually sick, and they did not know it. Unfortunately, the germs of sin have invaded all of us—religious and non-religious alike—and the only difference is the extent of the symptoms. Some sinners are easier to detect than others.

The Pharisees looked at themselves and said, "We are well. We are spiritually healthy!" Then they looked at Matthew's guests and said, "These people are sick!" Religious people today make the same mistake. This is why so many church members refuse to trust Jesus Christ: they think He came only for the down-and-out crowd and that they have no need of His ministry.

Jesus did not come to call the righteous, *because there are no righteous*. "There is none righteous, no, not one" (Rom. 3:10). There are all kinds of sinners just as there are all kinds of diseased people. All of them are sick, but the symptoms differ. The sinners in Matthew's house showed their spiritual sickness by rebelling against the Law, but the Pharisees showed their sickness by being proud of outwardly keeping the Law, yet breaking it in their hearts.

Jesus diagnoses sin and He performs a perfect cure. By His grace and power, He forgives sins and gives a new heart. When the Lord called Matthew and saved him, it was not a mere surface experience—it was a radical change in his life. The life of God entered into him and he became a new person.

As the Physician, Jesus Christ makes a perfect diagnosis, effects a perfect cure, and *pays the bill Himself*! I am sure there are many dedicated doctors and nurses who have aided people and never received payment. But no one has ever paid the kind of price that Jesus paid: He died for the patients. Salvation is a free gift because Jesus Christ purchased it for us on the cross.

There are two patients that Jesus Christ cannot heal of their sin sickness: the one who will not admit he is sick, and the one who will not trust Him for the cure. But those who admit their need and come to Him by faith receive His salvation.

He Is the Bridegroom Who Came to Bring Joy (Luke 5:33–35)

Jesus used the illustration of a bridegroom to answer the question of the disciples of John the Baptist. John was in prison at this time because he had rebuked Herod for his sins (Matt. 14:1–5). He still had many disciples, however, who had not yet gone over to follow Jesus. It is likely that the Pharisees were behind this question because they wanted to cause a breach between Jesus and John.

The Jews were required to fast only once a year, on the Day of Atonement (Lev. 23:27–29). The Pharisees thought that there was merit in much fasting, so they fasted twice a week (Luke 18:12). While Jesus did not *command* His followers to fast, He did *instruct* them to do it to God and not for the praise of men (Matt. 6:16–18). The rabbis had added a number of fasts to the calendar so that the Jewish religion became a burden rather than a blessing (Acts 15:10).

Of itself, religion does not bring joy. The Pharisees were very religious people, yet they seemed to have no joy. In fact, they resented it when other people were joyful. A religion of rules and regulations, practiced to achieve status and praise, is only an invitation to slavery and misery. Either the Pharisees did not know this or would not admit it.

Jesus replied to the Pharisees by comparing Himself to a physician, and He answered the disciples of John by comparing Himself to a bridegroom. Keep in mind that a wedding was a major social event to the Jews—there was no such thing as a quiet wedding on their social calendar. A wedding was an invitation to feast and rejoice. The groom was treated like a king, and his bride was treated like a queen. The guests and members of the bridal party were expected to enjoy themselves and thus add to the joy of the bride and groom. Not to show joy was an insult to the family giving the wedding feast.

Jesus' comparison of salvation to getting married opens up a whole new area for thought. Paul used the same image: "Wherefore, my brethren, ye also are become dead to the Law by the body of Christ; that ye should be married to another, even to Him who is raised from the dead, that we should bring forth fruit unto God" (Rom. 7:4).

Marriage is a love relationship, and so is our salvation—God loved us and sent His Son to die for us. But it takes more than love to get married, for there must also be commitment. I have officiated at hundreds of weddings, and the key question in the ceremony is: "Will you . . . ?" It is not enough for the groom to *know* the bride in his mind, or to have special *feelings* for her in his heart. He must *by an act of his own will* take her as his wife, and she must reciprocate.

Salvation involves much more than knowing *facts* about Jesus Christ, or even having special *feelings* toward Jesus Christ. Salvation comes to us when, by an act of the will, we receive Christ as our Saviour and Lord. I knew a great deal about the Lord before I was saved. I had faithfully attended Sunday School and had even been confirmed. There were times when I had religious feelings about Christ and even lifted my hand to ask for prayer. But it was not until I said "I will" to the prompting of His Holy Spirit that the transaction was completed. And all of this was by His grace. Even my willing was the result of His willing, for "it does not depend on the man who wills or the man who runs, but on God who has mercy" (Rom. 9:16).

Marriage begins with love and leads to joy. How can the wedding guests be miserable when they are sharing in such wonderful joy? When you are "married to Christ" you can experience the joy of sins forgiven, the joy of answered prayer, the joy of fellowship, the joy of service, and the joy of bringing forth "fruit unto God" (Rom. 7:4). Just as a bride may look forward to being fruitful and bearing children, so a Christian longs to be fruitful to the glory of God.

If a person professes to be a Christian and does not experience joy, either he is not saved or is out of fellowship with the Lord. The Christian life is a wedding feast, not a funeral! True, our Bridegroom is separated from us, and there are times of fasting and testing, but we look forward to seeing Him when He returns.

It is too bad that the average person on the street sees such poor examples of Christian living that he thinks trusting Christ means the end of your enjoyment. He needs to be told that God gives us "richly all things to enjoy" (1 Tim. 6:17). Religion can make a man miserable, but salvation brings him joy.

He Is the Transformer: He Came to Bring the New, Not to Patch Up the Old (Luke 5:35–39)

In these days of sanforized fabrics, and glass and plastic bottles, the illustration about cloth and wine-skins may confuse some. The Jews did not have pre-shrunk cloth for their clothing, and they frequently kept their liquids in skins. If a woman sewed a patch on a garment that had already been washed, the next time it was washed the patch would shrink and ruin both the patch and the garment. If new wine was poured into dry, brittle skins, the pressure of the gas from the fermentation would break the skin and the wine would be lost.

With these illustrations, Christ taught how to relate the old and the new. Many churches today refuse anything new, and as a consequence lack the joy and power that God has for them. Other churches accept every new thing that comes along and, in the process, destroy the old things that must be preserved.

The Pharisees resisted change. The Lord was a threat to them because He released a new life in those who trusted Him. In their zeal to be conservative the

Pharisees became "preservative" and fought the very doctrines they needed to believe. They had so embalmed their traditions that the people could not find the living Word of God.

Matthew and his friends had just received a new life, and they needed to know how to relate that life to the old truths of the Jewish faith. The disciples of John the Baptist were caught between these two groups. John had come as a reformer, putting the ax to the old and pointing to the new. Jesus and John were very different from each other—one a prophet of judgment, the other a Messenger of hope and salvation. John lived in the desert while Jesus was the Friend of publicans and sinners.

Jesus was neither a conformer (like the Pharisees) nor a reformer (like John the Baptist). He was (and is) a Transformer. He does not reject either the old or the new: *He transforms the old so that it is fulfilled in the new*. "Think not that I am come to destroy the Law, or the prophets; I am not come to destroy, but to fulfill" (Matt. 5:17).

If I have an acorn, I can destroy it in one of two ways. I can put it on the sidewalk and beat it to a pulp with a hammer. Or, I can plant it in the ground where it will die and produce an oak tree. The acorn would be destroyed by being fulfilled.

Jesus did not come to patch up the old, worn out Jewish religion. He came to fulfill it in His life, teaching, and death and resurrection. *He transformed the old by fulfilling it in the new*. To put new cloth on an old garment would destroy both. To put new wine in brittle wineskins would destroy both. To try to mix Law and Grace, Moses and Christ, would destroy both. But to permit the Law to be fulfilled in Grace, and Moses to be fulfilled in Christ, is what God accomplished.

Remember the illustration of the physician. How does the physician heal the human body? By helping the body heal itself. Although we have artificial aids for health, such as false teeth, pace-makers, and plastic arteries, the principle still remains that the human body must renew itself. Your body today is not the same as it was yesterday. New cells, millions of them, are constantly being manufactured. The new comes out of the old.

What about the wedding illustration? Do the bride and groom destroy their former homes? Of course not. The old is fulfilled in the new. The old generation gives birth to the new generation and that generation in turn gives birth to the next. There is continuity without conformity. The new home is like the old homes, and yet it is different. Every baby born may seem like every other baby, yet he is different.

Transformation comes from the inside out, the result of life within, not force without. When the Jewish nation refused the Gospel and rejected Christ, they were saying, "The old is better." (People are slow to change!) The Book of Hebrews was written to show them that the *new* is better, and that the new has grown out of the old.

When you trust Jesus Christ, He does not do a partial job of patching up your life. He comes into your life and transforms you from within. Paul wrote, "Therefore if any man be in Christ, he is a new creature: old things are passed away; behold, all things are become new" (2 Cor. 5:17). Religion may patch up a few weak spots in your life, but it cannot give you the new life that transforms.

When Christ comes into your life, it is not a temporary thing that will vanish at the next crisis. The patches were satisfactory until the garment got dirty and had to be washed, but then they fell apart and destroyed the garment. The wine was safe in the old wineskins until the gasses began to form. When the pressure increased, the skins were torn and the wine was spilled.

Salvation is not partial, temporary, or mixed. You are not saved by Jesus Christ *plus* Moses, or John the Baptist, or anybody else. The Pharisees wanted Jesus to compromise with them and He refused. He rejected their man-made traditions. He restored the living Word of God to the people, and He taught them that this Word was fulfilled in Himself.

There is something about us that resists change. "As it was in the beginning" is the theme song of many churches. Instead of our churches ministering as transforming fellowships, they muddle along monitoring conformity, and branding as heretics all who long to see the wind of the Spirit blow in fresh transforming power. To be sure, we must beware of "false fire," but we must also beware of painted fire. God expects us to walk "in newness of life" (Rom. 6:4). This means a fresh vital experience with Him day by day. There is always "something old, something new" because the new grows out of the old by the transforming power of Jesus Christ.

Have You Met Yourself in This Parable?

1. What is your attitude toward change?

2. Can you honestly say you have a "newness-of-life" experience with Jesus Christ?

3. Is your fellowship with Christ a feast or a funeral? Do you resent joyful Christians?

4. Is the fellowship in your church conservative or "preservative"? Are you looking at the future in a rearview mirror?

5. What part do you play in bringing life to your church and to the lives of others?

Luke 7:36–50

³⁶And one of the Pharisees desired Him that He would eat with him. And He went into the Pharisee's house, and sat down to meat. ³⁷And, behold, a woman in the city, which was a sinner, when she knew that Jesus sat at meat in the Pharisee's house, brought an alabaster box of ointment, ³⁸and stood at His feet behind Him weeping and began to wash His feet with hairs of her head, and kissed His feet, and anointed them with the ointment. ³⁹Now when the Pharisee which had bidden Him saw it, he spake within himself, saying, "This man, if He were a prophet, would have known who and what manner of woman this is that toucheth Him: for she is a sinner." ⁴⁰And Jesus answering said unto him, "Simon, I have somewhat to say unto thee." And he saith, "Master, say on." ⁴¹"There was a certain creditor which had two debtors: the one owed five hundred pence and the other fifty. ⁴²And when they had nothing to pay, he frankly forgave them both. Tell me therefore, which of them will love him most?" ⁴³Simon answered and said, "I suppose that he, to whom he forgave most." And He said unto him, "Thou hast rightly judged." ⁴⁴And He turned to the woman, and said unto Simon, "Seest thou this woman? I entered into thine house, thou gavest Me no water for My feet: but she hath washed My feet with tears, and wiped them with the hairs of her head. ⁴⁵Thou gavest me no kiss: but this woman since the time I came in hath not ceased to kiss my feet. ⁴⁶My head with oil thou didst not anoint: but this woman hath anointed My feet with ointment. ⁴⁷Wherefore I say unto thee, Her sins, which are many, are forgiven; for she loved much: but to whom little is forgiven, the same loveth little." ⁴⁸And He said unto her, "Thy sins are forgiven." ⁴⁹And they that sat at meat with Him began to say within themselves, "Who is this that forgiveth sins also?" ⁵⁰And He said to the woman, "Thy faith hath saved thee; go in peace."

4
Facts about Forgiveness
The Parable of the Two Debtors

Three miracles are recorded in Luke 7: A *great* miracle, the healing of the centurion's servant; a *greater* miracle, the raising of a young man from the dead; and the *greatest* miracle of all, the forgiving and restoring of a sinful woman. I believe that saving a lost sinner is the greatest miracle our Lord ever performs. After all, *it meets the greatest need*. God can heal the body and the person become ill again and eventually die, but salvation lasts for eternity. Forgiveness *produces the greatest results*—changed lives that glorify God. But most of all, forgiveness *required the greatest price*. It costs very little for God to heal the sick, but it cost His Son's death on a cross for Him to save the lost.

Why Simon the Pharisee invited Jesus to his home for a meal we do not know. Perhaps it was mere curiosity. After all, Jesus was popular, a great Teacher and miracle-Worker. Perhaps it was concern about what Christ's ministry meant to his own religious profession. It may be that Simon wanted to criticize, to find some fault with Jesus. Whatever Simon's motive, this much is certain: the dinner did not turn out quite the way he had planned.

When you or I give a dinner we invite our guests

and shut everybody else out. But this was not the custom in our Lord's day. The invited guests would lie on cushions around the table, while outsiders would come and go and even greet the guests. The host would provide cushions around the room so that any visitor could stop in and converse with the other people. This explains how the woman could so easily enter the banquet hall and how she had access to our Lord's feet for the anointing.

The appearance of this woman was certainly an embarrassment to Simon. But Jesus used her interruption to teach some important lessons about forgiveness.

We All Need Forgiveness

The Pharisee and the woman (who was known to be immoral) illustrate different kinds of sins and the fact that everyone sins and needs God's forgiveness.

1. *Sins of the flesh and sins of the spirit.* Simon was not guilty of immorality, but he was still a sinner. In the Sermon on the Mount (Matt. 5—7) and in Matthew 23, our Lord rebuked the Pharisees for their self-righteousness and unwillingness to admit their sins. They were guilty of hypocrisy and pride. They condemned others in order to exalt themselves. They were covetous, not only of money, but even more of prestige and praise. They practiced their religion only to be seen of men.

We must not get the idea that Jesus approved of immorality and disapproved of hypocrisy. He admitted that the woman was a sinner (vv. 47–48). She was guilty of gross sins of the flesh, but Simon was guilty of sins of the spirit. The late British Bible expositor, Dr. G. Campbell Morgan called these "the sins in good standing." They are with us today.

2. *Sins of commission and sins of omission.* Simon

knew what the woman had done, but forgot what he himself *had not done*. He had not even shown Jesus the common courtesies of the home—the kiss of welcome, water for His feet, and oil for His head. It is too bad that this woman fell into sin, but it is even worse that Simon was living in sin *and did not know it*. The person who does not do what God requires is just as guilty as the person who does what God forbids.

3. *Open sins and hidden sins*. Everyone at the feast knew who the woman was and what she had done with her life. Her sins were open. But only Jesus (who can read men's hearts) knew the sins in Simon's life. One of the words for sin in the Bible means "to miss the mark." Simon had missed the mark, even though he thought he had arrived. In the final judgment, it does not matter what *I* see in my life, or what *others* see; but it does matter what God sees.

It is important to realize that we are sinners *whether we feel guilty or not*. That is the whole point of the parable of the two debtors (Luke 7:41–43). Both of the men were in debt and were bankrupt. The difference between 500 pence and 50 pence is not a difference in guilt, for if we disobey in only one of God's laws we are guilty. The two amounts represent a difference in their *sense of guilt*. The woman was not more lost than the Pharisee. She only felt her guilt and need for mercy far more than Simon did. (Jesus illustrated this same truth in His parable of the Pharisee and publican, Luke 18:9–14.)

It is interesting to note that the people who walked closest to the Lord saw their sinfulness as the greatest. Abraham considered himself "but dust and ashes" (Gen. 18:27). God considered Job to be "perfect and upright" (Job 1:1) yet Job confessed to the Lord, "Behold, I am vile" (Job 40:4). Ezra, the godly scribe, prayed, "O my God, I am ashamed and blush to lift up my face" (Ezra 9:6). Peter fell to his knees and begged the Lord, "Depart from me, for I am a sinful man" (Luke 5:8), and when the Apostle John saw the glorified Christ, he fell at His feet as though he were a dead man (Rev. 1:17). The Apostle Paul called himself the chief of sinners (1 Tim. 1:15).

In the Bible, leprosy is sometimes used as a picture of sin. We now know that leprosy attacks the nerves so that the victim no longer feels. If he is injured in some way, there is no pain to warn him. Consequently, infection sets in and the limb starts to die. Sin has a similar deadening effect. I remember a man saying to me, "If this floor opened up and I dropped into hell, it wouldn't bother me one bit!"

Thank God for people like the unnamed woman, who feel their need and come to the Saviour! We cannot help but pity people like Simon, who proudly say, "I am rich, and increased with goods, and have need of nothing." To them, the Lord replies: "You know not that you are wretched, and miserable, and poor, and blind, and naked" (Rev. 3:17).

Forgiveness Is the Gracious Gift of God
Forgiveness is the greatest miracle God ever performs. Notice what is involved in this miracle.

1. It is all of grace. "He frankly forgave them both" (v. 42). This same word is translated "freely give" in Romans 8:32 and "freely given" in 1 Corinthians 2:12. Forgiveness is not something we may purchase or earn, because we are bankrupt—we have nothing with which to pay. Paul wrote, "For by grace are ye saved through faith; and that not of yourselves; it is the gift of God (Eph. 2:8).

The concept of grace was difficult for the Pharisees to understand because theirs was a religion of merit through good works. The Pharisee in another parable boasted of his good character and conduct: "God, I thank Thee, that I am not as other men are, extortioners, unjust, adulterers, or even as this publican. I fast twice in the week, I give tithes of all that I possess" (Luke 18:11–12).

The concept of grace is difficult for people to understand even today. Evangelist D. L. Moody had spent many days studying what the Bible taught about the grace of God, and he was so excited about what he had learned that he went out into the street, stopped the first man he met, and asked, "What do you know about grace?" Startled by this approach, the stranger replied, "Grace? Grace who?" Then Mr. Moody told him about the grace of God.

The only way sinners can be saved is by God's grace, for they are too bankrupt to purchase or earn salvation any other way. "For God hath concluded them all in unbelief, that He might have mercy upon all" (Rom. 11:32).

2. Forgiveness is received by faith. The woman's tears did not save her, for no amount of remorse or repentance can save the soul. August Toplady wrote:

> Could my zeal no respite know,
> Could my tears forever flow,
> All for sin could not atone,
> Thou must save and Thou alone.

Unless repentance is joined with faith in Christ, it leads to even greater guilt and condemnation.

According to the Gospel harmonies, the event that just preceded this feast was Christ's great invitation to sinners, "Come unto Me, all ye that labor and are heavy laden, and I will give you rest. Take My yoke upon you, and learn of Me; for I am meek and lowly in heart: and ye shall find rest unto your souls. For My yoke is easy, and My burden is light" (Matt. 11:28–

30). I wonder if that sinful woman did not hear this gracious Word and right then and there trust Jesus Christ? We know that she was already saved when she entered the banquet hall, for Jesus said to her, "Thy sins are forgiven" (v. 48), and the tense of the Greek verb means "They have been forgiven, they are forgiven, and they stand forgiven." What was it that accomplished this miracle? Jesus said, "Thy faith hath saved thee" (v. 50).

A careless reading of verse 47 would give the false impression that people are saved by love. We hear a great deal about love these days, and get the idea that many people think God saves sinners because of some good feeling they have down inside. But *nobody is saved by God's love*. God loves the whole world (John 3:16) and yet the whole world is not saved. Sinners are saved *by grace* through faith in Jesus Christ. It was this woman's *faith* that saved her. She heard God's Word ("Come unto Me"), responded to God's invitation, trusted God's Son, and experienced God's forgiveness.

We are not saved by faith in faith. We are saved by faith in Jesus Christ and Him alone. How do we know we can trust Him? His Word assures us, "So then faith cometh by hearing, and hearing by the word of God" (Rom. 10:17). I once heard a man pray, "Lord, may many sinners here *transfer* their faith to Jesus Christ." That spoke to me. Everybody has faith in something. The difference between a Christian and a lost sinner is not that the Christian has faith and the lost sinner does not. The difference is in *the object of faith*. When you transfer your faith to Jesus Christ, it becomes *saving* faith.

3. *Forgiveness is certain*. Jesus gave assurance to this woman before He sent her away. She heard Him say to Simon, "Her sins . . . are forgiven" (v.47), and

He said directly to her, "Thy sins are forgiven" (v. 48). If you had asked her a week later, "How do you know you are saved?" she would have replied, "Jesus said so." How do people *today* know they are saved? The Word of God says so: "These things have I written unto you that believe on the name of the Son of God; that ye may know that ye have eternal life" (1 John 5:13).

Suppose this woman had depended on her own feelings for assurance. While she was near Jesus, weeping and expressing her love, she would have felt saved. But a few hours later, when she had calmed down, and when the tears of joy had stopped, would she have felt the same way? Probably not. You dare not depend on feelings alone for the assurance of salvation.

If the woman had based her assurance on the words and attitudes of the people around her she would have had very little assurance. The guests shunned her and Simon criticized her. While we appreciate the encouragement we receive from others, we dare not build our assurance on this alone. Peter thought that all of the twelve apostles were saved (John 6:69), and the Jerusalem saints, including the leaders, were not sure Paul was a converted man (Acts 9:26–27).

Feelings change, but God's Word never changes. People make mistakes, but God's Word is always true. The assurance of salvation must come from the Word of God, witnessed by the Spirit of God (Rom. 8:9).

4. Forgiveness is costly. In the parable of the two debtors, the creditor took a loss. Since the debtors were bankrupt and he "frankly forgave them," he had to pay the price of their debt. Salvation is free, but it is not cheap. It cost Jesus Christ His life on the cross. I doubt that anyone in that banquet hall knew how much it cost Jesus to say to that woman, "Thy sins are forgiven." I wonder if any of them were at Calvary when He said, "Father, forgive them, for they know not what they do" (Luke 23:34).

I once had lunch with a very intelligent man who was a universalist. He believed that God would ultimately save everyone. "After all," he argued, "did not Jesus die for the sins of the whole world?" Of course He did. But there is a difference between the *efficiency* of His atonement (it is for all) and the *efficacy* of the atonement (it works only for those who will trust Him). A man who refuses help when the hotel he is staying in is burning down does not by his foolish act condemn the fireman—he condemns himself.

We all need forgiveness, and forgiveness is the gift of God.

Forgiveness Results in a Changed Life

The woman's faith in Christ changed her. The condemnation and terror of the Law did not make her a new person, nor did the religious system of the Pharisees. It was the grace of God. "Therefore, if any man [or woman] is in Christ, he is a new creature; the old things passed away; behold, new things have come" (2 Cor. 5:17, NASB). What are some of the new things that characterized her changed life?

1. New love. An old Welsh proverb says, "In every pardon there is love." A hardened criminal may not love the governor and the judge who pardon him, but the condemned sinner certainly loves God when he experiences His pardon and forgiveness. When you feel great guilt as a sinner, you experience great love as a saint. This helps to explain why the Apostle Paul loved Christ so much: he knew how guilty he was as an unconverted sinner.

Love for Christ and love for others is evidence of having been forgiven. "If God were your Father, ye would love Me" Jesus told His enemies (John 8:42). Paul boldly wrote to the Corinthians, "If any man love not the Lord Jesus Christ, let him be Anathema [accursed]" (1 Cor. 16:22).

The woman was not ashamed to show her love for Christ openly. People were watching, and some of them were embarrassed, but she went right on anointing Him and kissing His feet. Many citizens of Chicago called D. L. Moody "Crazy Moody" because of his enthusiastic love for Christ and lost souls, but history has vindicated Mr. Moody's faith and love. God displayed His love for us openly at Calvary (Rom. 5:8), so why should we be timid about openly showing our love for Him?

The woman displayed her love devotedly and sacrificially. The Greek verbs indicate that she *repeatedly* anointed His feet, kissed them, and wiped them with her hair. It was not a quick once-and-for-all action, like a nervous teenager kissing his grandmother goodbye! No doubt the ointment was expensive— she did not give Him something that cost her nothing (1 Chron. 21:22–25). She had not received cheap forgiveness and she did not bring cheap worship.

It is worth noting that this woman devoted to Christ all that previously she had used for sin. The harlot used kisses, beauty, and spices to lead men into sin (Prov. 7:6ff), but the forgiven woman gave all of these to her Saviour.

2. *New freedom*. The Lord sent the woman away, wearing His easy yoke. She had been wearing the heavy yoke of sin, in bondage to the sins of the flesh. But Jesus had forgiven her, and forgiveness always leads to freedom. "If the Son therefore shall make you free, ye shall be free indeed" (John 8:36). Sin

promises freedom but always brings bondage. The cords of sin are woven gradually, but they are woven with strength.

Simon the Pharisee had no freedom because there is none in the yoke of religious legalism. He pitied the woman, yet he should have pitied himself.

3. *New peace*. Because she was forgiven, this woman had peace with God. Jesus said, "Thy faith hath saved thee; go in peace" (v. 50). Isaiah declared, "'There is no peace,' saith the Lord, 'unto the wicked'" (Isa. 48:22). There can be no peace without righteousness. "And the work of righteousness shall be peace; and the effect of righteousness quietness and assurance forever" (Isa. 32:17). "Therefore, being justified by faith, we have peace with God through our Lord Jesus Christ" (Rom. 5:1).

Literally, Luke 7:50 reads, "Go *into* peace." It is as though peace is the realm into which she walked and she lived day by day. Grace and faith lead to peace, and peace is the spiritual atmosphere of the believer. Christ said "Go into peace" to two persons, both of them women. He spoke it to the woman in Simon's house, and He spoke it to the woman who touched the hem of His garment (Luke 8:48). He speaks that word today to any who will trust Him for salvation.

The woman went out a changed person. Simon the Pharisee could have become a changed person too but he missed his opportunity. His problem was *spiritual blindness*. To begin with, Simon did not see *himself*. He thought he was a righteous person, acceptable to God, when in reality he was bankrupt and condemned. He saw the sins of other people but could not see his own sins. He did not even realize how discourteously he had treated Christ.

Simon really did not see *the woman*. He saw only her past. Jesus Christ saw her present and future.

Simon saw only the outside, but the Lord saw her heart.

The basic reason for Simon's blindness was that he did not really see *the Lord Jesus Christ*. He called Him "Teacher" (v. 40, NASB), but in his heart was saying, "This man, if he were a prophet . . ." (v. 39). Until we know Jesus Christ personally, we can never have our spiritual eyes opened to see ourselves and others.

Have You Met Yourself in This Parable?

1. How would you respond if a disreputable person came uninvited to a party you were hosting?

2. How big is your debt—500 or 50 pence?

3. Do you ever feel as though you have sufficient means to pay your debt?

4. Can others see in your actions your love for Christ?

5. Are you guilty of judging and condemning others whom Christ has forgiven and accepted?

6. Are you enjoying the *freedom* and *peace* of His forgiveness?

Luke 10:25–37

[25]And, behold a certain lawyer stood up, and tempted Him, saying, "Master, what shall I do to inherit eternal life?" [26]He said unto him, "What is written in the Law? How readest thou?" [27]And he answering said, "Thou shalt love the Lord thy God with all thy heart, and with all thy soul, and with all thy strength, and with all thy mind; and thy neighbor as thyself." [28]And He said unto him, "Thou hast answered right: this do, and thou shalt live." [29]But he, willing to justify himself, said unto Jesus, "And who is my neighbor?" [30]And Jesus answering said, "A certain man went down from Jerusalem to Jericho, and fell among thieves, which stripped him of his garment, and wounded him, and departed, leaving him half dead. [31]And by chance there came down a certain priest that way: and when he saw him, he passed by on the other side. [32]And likewise a Levite, when he was at the place, came and looked on him, and passed by on the other side. [33]But a certain Samaritan, as he journeyed, came where he was: and when he saw him, he had compassion on him, [34]and went to him, and bound up his wounds, pouring in oil and wine, and set him on his own beast, and brought him to an inn, and took care of him. [35]And on the morrow when he departed, he took out two pence, and gave them to the host, and said unto him, 'Take care of him; and whatsoever thou spendest more, when I come again, I will repay thee.' [36]Which now of these three, thinkest thou, was neighbor unto him that fell among thieves?" [37]And he said, "He that showed mercy on him." Then said Jesus unto him, "Go, and do thou likewise."

5
Learning to Care Enough
The Parable of the Good Samaritan

The ingredients that make up the familiar story of the Good Samaritan are found on the pages of daily newspapers. There is really nothing new under the sun. In this story, Christ talked about violence—and we certainly have plenty of that today. He talked about crime, racial discrimination, and hatred. In this parable we see neglect and unconcern, but we also see love and mercy. The person who says the Bible is not relevant to our modern world has never read this parable.

We know what the parable *says*, but what does it *mean?* Some of the ancient scholars tried to make everything in this story symbolize something, but this approach took them on a detour. The story was given because a lawyer (an expert in Jewish law) asked Jesus, "And who is my neighbor?" He was really trying to rescue himself from losing an argument, but Jesus used his question as an opportunity to teach an important truth, namely, *you cannot separate your relationship with God from your relationship with your fellowman.*

Consider the persons involved in this story and the different attitudes they had toward the man who journeyed from Jerusalem to Jericho.

The Thieves: He was a Victim to Exploit

When the thieves saw the man traveling down the road, they did not see a fellow human being or a creature made in the image of God. They saw someone they could exploit. It did not matter how they harmed him, so long as they got what they wanted. Their philosophy was, "What's yours is mine—I'll take it!"

A friend of mine is a successful insurance salesman and an effective witness for Christ. He told me one day, "I really have to pray for the Lord's help to keep Christ first in my business relationships. Every time I meet a new friend, my tendency is to ask, 'I wonder how much insurance he has?' instead of 'I wonder if he is born again?'" I know a girl who broke up with her boyfriend because he used every social engagement to push his merchandise rather than to meet her friends and have a good time.

God gave us *things* to use and *people* to love. If we start *loving* things, we will start *using* people, and this is exploitation. If we take from others, but fail to give in some way, we are exploiting. It is easy for parents to use their children and tear them down instead of build them up. "I'm not a child in this family," a bitter teenage girl told me. "I'm the assistant mother. I stay home and work so my mother can run around and have fun." It was no surprise when that girl left home and eventually broke her parents' hearts. She had been exploited.

It is even possible to exploit people in the name of religion. I have met pastors and Sunday School workers who, just to make themselves look good, have used church members in various programs. True Christian service builds the worker while it builds the church.

Jesus Christ never exploits a person. He always

gives back more than He asks. He always leaves a
person in better shape than when He found him. If
He wounds, He always heals. The Lord considers the
worker more important than the work. This explains
why He spent so much time with the Prophet Jonah.

We must beware of looking at someone and asking
ourselves, "What I can get out of him?" This is the
same attitude the thieves had. We may not brutally
beat other people and wound their bodies, but we
may hurt them with words and attitudes.

The Priest and Levite: He Was a Nuisance to Avoid
Jericho was a priestly city, so the priests and Levites
would often be on the road that led from Jerusalem to
Jericho. This being true, you wonder why that road
remained so dangerous. Certainly, the religious
leaders could have done something to clean up the
crime in that area. But even apart from the neighborhood problem, you would have expected these two
religious workers to do something for the victim at the
side of the road. Instead, they passed by on the other
side.

I can think of a number of reasons (or excuses) these
men could have given to defend their conduct.
Perhaps you and I have used one or more of them to
defend our lack of love and concern.

*"I've been serving at the temple. I've done my
part."* How strange that one form of spiritual work
should compete with another! Too many Christians
excuse personal ministry to the needy on the grounds
that they hold a church office or serve on a committee.

"I've been away from home and need to hurry."
The priests' service was divided into 24 courses and
they served according to a plan so they would not be
away from home constantly. It may have been a

sacrifice for the priest and Levite to serve at the temple, but no sacrifice is a substitute for compassionate service. Jesus said, "I will have mercy and not sacrifice" (Matt. 9:13).

"It's not my fault." But maybe it was. Why didn't the religious leaders do something about that dangerous road? Cain asked, "Am I my brother's keeper?" (Gen. 4:9) And the answer is, "Yes, regardless of your brother's race or color." If being a Christian does not make me a better human being, there is something wrong with my Christianity.

"Let somebody else do it." The priest could have said, "Well, the Levite is coming behind me, so I'll let him do it." And when the Levite showed up, he could have said, "The priest didn't do anything, so why should I?" You and I can always find somebody to point to as an excuse for our own neglect. Failure to do a *good* thing is as sinful as actually doing a *bad* thing. James wrote, "Therefore, to him that knoweth to do good and doeth it not, to him it is sin" (James 4:17).

If we go through life wanting to have our own way then people who need us will be nuisances to us. But if we go through life seeking to share the love of Christ, every "nuisance" will become an opportunity for ministry to glorify God.

The Lawyer: He Was a Problem to Discuss

I realize that Christ did not include either the lawyer or the inn host in His application, because He asked, "Which now of these three . . ." (v. 36), but I want to include them because they help us better understand ourselves.

The lawyer, of course, was an expert in Old Testament law. He was a professional theologian, trained to examine the Word of God and apply it to daily life. One of the stock questions the lawyers discussed in that day was, "What shall a man do to inherit eternal life?" He asked Jesus that question, hoping to trip Him up in an argument, but the Lord was too wise for him. Rather than admit defeat, the lawyer tried to escape with an academic discussion of definitions: "Who is my neighbor?" Our modern lawyers still use the same device: "Define what you mean by that term."

One of the best ways to get nothing done is to discuss it. We think we have solved a problem or met a need because we have held a committee meeting! Discussing has become a substitute for doing. We have conferences about crime, and crime continues to grow. We have seminars about education, and the average student is still unable to read or write correctly. Churches and denominations conduct expensive conventions about winning a lost world, and still very few church members make any attempt to witness to their neighbors.

D. L. Moody believed in getting things done. One day he and his musician, Ira Sankey, stood on a street corner in Indianapolis, Indiana. While Sankey sang, Moody gathered a crowd. Then he got on the soap box and preached a sermon to an interested audience of men on their way home from work. When he thought the crowd was large enough, he led them down the street to the opera house, and preached to them again. He looked at his watch and said, "I must now close the meeting. There is going to be a convention here in a few minutes to discuss the subject, 'How to reach the masses.'"

The lawyer wanted to talk about the abstract theme of neighborliness. Jesus pulled him down to a concrete incident about a man who had been beaten and robbed. It is easy to discuss general topics but it is hard to get involved in specific needs. The lawyer felt safer discussing theories—he was nervous when it came to personal applications. He failed to see that the important question was not "Who is my neighbor?" but "To whom can I be a neighbor?"

How easy it is to be like this lawyer and substitute law for love! We obey a rule and think we have served God. We explain a doctrine and think we have grown spiritually. We are comfortable spectators and not concerned participants. People in need are not problems to discuss. They are people who need our love and ministry. Talking about needs may be necessary, but talking must never be a substitute for doing.

The Inn Host: He Was a Customer to Serve

I do not criticize the host for not being on the road to help the victim. He had his inn to manage, and that would keep him busy. But I want to use the host to illustrate the fact that many Christians serve other people only because it is their job and they are paid to do it. Perhaps the host would have assisted the victim even without the payment that the Samaritan gave him. But there are other people who will not lift a finger to serve their fellowman until they have heard the right answer to their question, "What am I going to get out of it?"

Motive has a great deal to do with ministry. It is possible to do a good thing with a bad motive. The Pharisees prayed, gave offerings, and fasted—all of which are acceptable religious practices—but their motive was to gain the praise of men, not to give glory to God. This robbed them of true and lasting blessing. If I serve you *only* because I am being paid to do it, then I am treating you like a customer, not a person who needs love and care.

The offices in a local church are usually filled by volunteers who are elected or appointed by the congregation or church council. Nobody is paid for being a trustee or deacon or Sunday School teacher. For this reason, church officers must be careful to maintain spiritual motives. It is relatively easy to *fill* an office, but difficult to *use* an office. You will be criticized and you will have to do a lot of work alone. When your term of office ends, you probably will not receive the kind of appreciation you deserve from the people you have served.

All of which means we must never serve the Lord and His people with an opportunist attitude. If we do, we will be disappointed and unhappy. But if we serve in love, seeking to please Jesus Christ, then we will have satisfaction and blessing. And you can be sure that, when He returns, Jesus Christ will reward you for all you have done in His name.

Of the five attitudes demonstrated in this passage only one was right, and it belonged to the Samaritan.

The Samaritan: He Was a Neighbor to Serve

When Christ uttered the phrase "But a certain Samaritan . . ." I am sure His Jewish listeners were startled. A Samaritan! The Jews had no dealings with the Samaritans (John 4:9). In his daily morning prayer, the proud Pharisee thanked God he had not been born a woman, a Gentile, or a Samaritan, and some Pharisees prayed that the Samaritans would be excluded from the resurrection. A *Gentile* could become a Jewish proselyte, but not a *Samaritan*.

How did this family feud get started? In 722 B.C. the northern kingdom of Israel was taken captive by Assyria. Some 20,000 Jews were deported and an equivalent number of foreigners moved in to take their place. This led to a mingling of the Jews and

Gentiles so that the children of these marriages were a mixed race. The pure Jews refused to have anything to do with these Samaritans, so the Samaritans established their own temple, priesthood, and religious ceremonies. They claimed that Mount Gerizim, not Mount Zion, was God's appointed place for worship.

The last person you would expect to help a Jew would be a Samaritan, yet this is the very person Christ selected for His parable. The Samaritan did not permit either racial or religious barriers to hinder him from helping the Jewish victim. Whether the victim would have protested or not, we do not know. When you are half-dead, you forget your prejudices in a hurry. The Samaritan did not blame the injured man for the collective attitudes of either race and use that as an excuse to do nothing. He dared to act as a concerned individual. Notice the elements involved in his ministry to the victim.

1. Compassion (10:33). This is much more than passing pity. The Greek word for compassion carries the idea of the inner being deeply moved and stirred. It is the word used to describe our Lord's feelings when He beheld lost sinners (Matt. 9:36; 14:14; 15:32; 18:27). It is this kind of love that moves us to serve others and not think of ourselves.

It is interesting to note that the word translated "compassion" is generally used in the New Testament with reference to Jesus Christ. However, in three of His parables Christ uses the word with reference to people: in the parable of the Good Samaritan, in the story of the king who had compassion on the dishonest servant and forgave him (Matt. 18:23–25), and in the parable of the prodigal son (Luke 15:11–32), where the father saw his wayward son and had compassion on him.

Compassion describes the way God feels about us. When we show compassion to others, we are simply treating them the way God has treated us. "We love, because He first loved us" (1 John 4:19, NASB).

2. *Contact (10:34)*. The Samaritan could have excused himself by saying, "Those robbers may still be in the area. Perhaps they are using him as a decoy. I had better get out of here quickly!" Or he might have argued that the man was too far gone, or that there was little he could do. But he did not try to evade his responsibilities. Love does not look at obstacles—it looks at opportunities. The priest and Levite were unwilling to personally come into contact with the man, but the Samaritan did.

3. *Care (10:34)*. It is not enough that we have contact with our neighbor, or even that we show compassion—we must go a step farther and do something practical. The Samaritan cleansed the victim's wounds with wine, and then soothed them with oil. He bound up the wounds so they could begin to heal. He then took the man to the inn for further care and promised to return. The lawyer was willing to talk, but unwilling to act. The Samaritan acted, even though he was taking his own life in his hands.

4. *Cost (10:35)*. The Samaritan interrupted his schedule to care for the man. Did he perhaps lose a business opportunity because of this? Was he late to an appointment? We do not know, but we do know he was willing to give *time* to a needy stranger.

He shared his beast with the man and took him to an inn. He stayed there and nursed the patient, and paid the bill himself. What did he have to gain from this personally? Nothing—except the joy and growth that come when you live by love and serve others without expecting recognition or reward.

There is always a price to pay when you live by compassion. Dr. J. H. Jowett has said, "Ministry that costs nothing accomplishes nothing." Love is costly. It was costly for Christ and it will be costly for us. The Samaritan did not set up a committee and hire somebody else to minister to the Jericho Road victims. He did the work himself and paid the price from his own resources.

Of course, what the Samaritan did is surely a picture of what Jesus Christ has done for us. That is not the main lesson of the story, but it is a valid application. Christ found us as lost sinners on the road of life, half-dead, with nobody to care. Men did not help us, religion could not help us, so He came to meet our needs. He came where we were, for He took upon Himself human flesh and entered this world as a human being. He had compassion on us and healed us, *and He paid the full price*. There was nothing in us that merited this salvation. It was all done because of His compassion for sinners.

Jesus Christ is not only the Saviour of lost sinners—He is also the Example for those who are saved. Just as He served others when He was here on earth, so should we. How easy it is for us to think only of those who belong to our group or those who can do something for us in return. Like the priest and Levite, we can quickly think up excuses for not getting involved. Like the lawyer, we can debate the abstract issues while we ignore the concrete cases right before our eyes.

That Jewish lawyer got the message. When Jesus asked him which of the three was neighbor to the victim—the priest, the Levite, or the Samaritan—the lawyer gave the correct answer, *but he would not use the word "Samaritan"*! He said, "He that showed mercy on him." You cannot help but think that there was still a pocket of resistance in his heart. He was holding fast to his prejudices.

A Great Deal of Difference

As you and I read and study this parable, we are likely to say: "All of this is very beautiful, but is it practical? What difference will it make in this whole world if one person helps another person?" It can make a great deal of difference. Jesus told this story centuries ago, and yet is has blessed and challenged millions of people ever since.

One act of ministry, motivated by Christian compassion, not only pleases the Lord and helps the needy—it also blesses the one ministering. The results go on forever. It is like dropping a stone in a puddle of water and seeing the ripples reach out in an ever-widening circle. The old familiar poem is true:

Only one life,
'Twill soon be past;
Only what's done for Christ
Will last.

Have You Met Yourself in This Parable?

1. With which of the characters in the story do you identify the most?

2. Have you ever felt like the victim, being exploited by others? How do you respond to this?

3. When you see or hear a need, what is your immediate response: excuses or ideas for helping?

4. Do you deal with the problems of life in the abstract or in concrete, practical ways? Is arguing or discussing problems a device you use to avoid taking responsibilities?

5. Does it really cost you anything to serve God?

6. What motivates your Christian life and service? Do you have and show true Christian compassion toward others?

Luke 11:1–13

¹And it came to pass, that, as He was praying in a certain place, when He ceased, one of His disciples said unto Him, "Lord, teach us to pray, as John also taught his disciples." ²And He said unto them, "When ye pray, say 'Our Father which art in heaven, Hallowed be Thy name. Thy kingdom come. Thy will be done, as in heaven, so in earth. ³Give us day by day our daily bread. ⁴And forgive us our sins; for we also forgive every one that is indebted to us. And lead us not into temptation; but deliver us from evil'." ⁵And He said unto them, "Which of you shall have a friend, and shall go unto him at midnight, and say unto him, 'Friend, lend me three loaves; ⁶for a friend of mine in his journey is come to me, and I have nothing to set before him?' ⁷And he from within shall answer and say, 'Trouble me not: the door is now shut, and my children are with me in bed; I cannot rise and give thee.' ⁸I say unto you, though he will not rise and give him, because he is his friend, yet because of his importunity he will rise and give him as many as he needeth. ⁹And I say unto you, Ask, and it shall be given you; seek, and ye shall find; knock, and it shall be opened unto you. ¹⁰For every one that asketh receiveth; and he that seeketh findeth; and to him that knocketh it shall be opened. ¹¹If a son shall ask bread of any of you that is a father, will he give him a stone? or if he ask a fish, will he for a fish give him a serpent? ¹²Or if he shall ask an egg, will he offer him a scorpion? ¹³If ye then, being evil, know how to give good gifts unto your children: how much more shall your heavenly Father give the Holy Spirit to them that ask Him?"

6
The School of Prayer
The Parable of the Friend at Midnight

No Christian rises any higher than his praying. Everything we are and everything we do for the Lord depends on prayer. Most of us would rather work than pray. But we know that without prayer our work is useless. What a difference it would make in our personal lives, our homes, our churches, and our world if Christians really learned to pray—*and prayed!*

If you had the privilege of asking the Lord for one specific blessing, would you ask, "Teach me to pray"? Someone may ask, "Lord, teach me how to make money!" or, "Lord, teach me how to preach." But "Teach me to pray" is the wisest request, because every other blessing in the Christian life depends in one way or another on our ability to pray.

The School of Prayer has four grades, and each grade emphasizes a particular lesson about prayer.

Grade School: We Must Pray (11:1)
We do not know which disciple asked to be enrolled in the School of Prayer, but we know he was a discerning man. He felt a need for effective prayer. He was praying about his praying. How many of us do that?

He was impressed with the fact that Jesus was a Man of prayer. There are at least 10 references to Jesus' prayer life in Luke's Gospel. Jesus was God manifest in human flesh, and yet He prayed. He was conceived by the Holy Spirit and filled with the Spirit, yet He prayed. He lived a sinless life and was always obedient to His Father's will, yet He had to pray. He had the power to perform miracles, yet He needed to pray.

If Jesus Christ had all of this in His favor, and yet had to pray, *how much more do you and I need to pray!* We have a human nature that is prone to sin. We often grieve the Spirit and sometimes rebel against our Father's gracious will. If our Lord needed to pray when He was on earth, then certainly you and I need to pray. That *we must pray* is the Grade School lesson in the School of Prayer.

John the Baptist also prayed. We think of him primarily as a prophet, but it is obvious that he was a mighty man of prayer. John was related to Jesus in the flesh, yet he had to pray. John was filled with the Spirit before he was born, yet he had to pray. John was the greatest of the prophets, yet he had to pray. So important was prayer to John's life and ministry that he taught his disciples to pray.

John the Baptist and Jesus were sent by the Father to accomplish His purpose. John was a Nazarite, forbidden to drink the fruit of the vine, while Jesus turned water into wine and even established a memorial meal that uses wine. John performed no miracles, while Jesus was recognized as a miracle Worker come from God. John was a recluse of the wilderness, but Jesus attended weddings, accepted invitations to meals, and even played with the babies. John's message was primarily one of judgment, while Christ preached God's mercy and grace. These two men seemed to have little in common, *yet both of them prayed and depended on prayer*.

A new believer discovers soon enough that he cannot live the Christian life successfully unless he prays. Prayer is not a luxury—it is a necessity. If the Son of God had to pray, and if a spiritual giant like John the Baptist had to pray, how much more do we need to pray! A Christian who claims to be getting along without prayer is only fooling himself. No Christian can get along without prayer, for prayer is to the inner man what breath is to the outer man. How long could you manage without breathing?

High School: We Must Pray in God's Will (11:2–4)

Nobody wants to stay in Grade School. The more we learn, the better we can live. This is true in the School of Prayer. The High School level is the next step, and here we discover that true prayer is simply asking *in the will of God*. A little child asks for anything and everything, and usually does not get what he asks for. The maturing child discovers what it is his father wants to give him, then asks for and receives it.

People make two mistakes about the Lord's Prayer. (Actually, this prayer should be called the Disciple's Prayer since it is obvious that our Lord could never pray it.) The first mistake is in thinking this prayer is the *only* prayer, that it must be memorized and repeated, and that there is a certain amount of blessing received each time you recite it. Nowhere in the Bible is this taught.

The second mistake goes to the other extreme. It is the idea that this prayer does not apply to believers today, that it belongs to some future period and therefore must not be used today. Since the parallel prayer is found in Matthew 6:9–13, and since Matthew is a Gospel written especially for the Jews, some students conclude that this prayer has no application to the church today. The fact that this prayer is in the Sermon on the Mount adds more weight to this view, since many Bible scholars claim the Sermon on the Mount does not apply to Christian believers today.

This is not the place to enter into an extended discussion of the matter. Suffice it to say that you can find parallels in the Epistles to the teaching Christ gives in the Sermon on the Mount. I can find nothing in either the Sermon on the Mount in general, or the Lord's Prayer in particular, that lies outside the experience of a Christian today. It is my conviction that this prayer teaches us how to pray *in the will of God*.

Robert Law wrote, "Prayer is a mighty instrument, not for getting man's will done in Heaven, but for getting God's will done on earth." Or, as other saints have expressed it "Prayer is not overcoming God's reluctance, but laying hold of His willingness." When you graduate into the High School level of praying you learn to pray in the will of God.

I believe the Lord's Prayer is a model for us to follow, not a form for us to recite. There is nothing wrong with reciting the Lord's Prayer, provided it comes from the heart and is not just a ritual. For that matter, *any* prayer could become an empty ritual. If you examine this prayer carefully, you will discover several principles that will help you pray in the will of God.

1. Prayer is based on relationship. "Our Father" expresses a dual relationship "Our" expresses my relationship to other Christians, and "Father" expresses my relationship to God. Unless I can honestly call God my Father, I cannot pray. Note too that there are *no singular pronouns in this prayer*. It is not "My Father . . . Give me . . . Forgive me . . . Lead me . . ." It is "Our Father . . . Give us . . . Forgive us . . . Lead us . . ." The prayer is a family prayer, involving the Father in heaven and His children on earth.

This leads to an important truth: Christians must want what the Father wants, not anything that would hurt His family. I have no right to ask God for a blessing that would in some way hurt you. Selfish praying will not receive the answer expected. For instance, the psalmist wrote, "And He gave them their request; but sent leanness into their souls" (Ps. 106:15)

2. *Prayer involves responsibilities.* Before we talk to God about *our* needs, we must focus on *His* concerns. What does God want to happen as the result of our praying? He wants His Name glorified. He wants His kingdom to come and His will to be done on earth. Anything in my praying that is not part of these tremendous issues is out of the will of God. Our heavenly Father does not answer prayer simply to make life easier for us. He answers prayer in order to accomplish His eternal purposes in our lives and on this earth. Prayer is the most important part of the advancement of God's program for His church. I have no right to ask God to rearrange His eternal plan just to make me happy. The thing that should make me the happiest is knowing that His will is being done and His name is being glorified.

3. *Prayer involves requests (Luke 11:3-4).* After we have put God's concerns first, then we can bring our requests to Him. There is a reason for this order: we find our own requests changing as we put the glory of God first in our praying. Many times I have come to God in prayer with what I thought were very serious matters. But as I yielded myself to His will, and as I

prayed that He would be glorified, these serious matters began to look less menacing. Prayer in the will of God helps give perspective to your life.

God is concerned about the needs that we have, but He wants us to relate those needs to His higher purposes. No need is too small or too great for God. We can claim His promises, such as Philippians 4:19, "And my God shall supply all your needs according to His riches in glory in Christ Jesus" and know that He will answer.

God will also forgive us and cleanse us as we confess our sins to Him (1 John 1:9). And He will guide us and guard us on the path of life as we ask Him and yield to His leading. He forgives yesterday's sins, He provides today's bread, and He directs in tomorrow's decisions. Every need that we have is met by our loving Father as we pray in His will.

College: We Must Pray as Children Coming to a Father (11:5–12)

This parable has been greatly misunderstood by many people, mainly because they do not understand middle eastern hospitality. Jesus told this story about friendship, but then shifted the emphasis to *sonship* (v. 11). True prayer is not based on our friendship with God, but on the fact that we are the *children* of God.

In a middle eastern village, hospitality is a very important thing. When a guest arrives, the whole village is involved in entertaining him. For the village not to entertain him would be a terrible breach of etiquette, and for the guest to refuse the hospitality would be a greater sin. Whether the visitor is hungry or not, he is offered food and must eat.

When Jesus described the sleeping neighbor as He did, His listeners must have been horrified, for no member of a village would ever refuse to help a guest. For the man to say "Trouble me not!" would be a violation of the social code and an insult to the entire village. You could paraphrase verse 5: "Can any of you imagine a friend . . ." because Jesus expected a negative reply, "No! We cannot think of one of our neighbors doing such a thing!"

In other words, the Lord is not comparing God to the sleeping neighbor; He is *contrasting* the two. He is saying, "If a sleeping neighbor, on the basis of friendship and social etiquette, will meet the needs of a friend, *how much more* will your Father in heaven meet the needs of His own children!" With this in mind, let's contrast the Father and the neighbor.

To begin with, our Father in heaven never slumbers or sleeps. He is always alert to our needs. We do not have to pound at His door to wake Him up. He knows our needs even before we know them. Furthermore, the Father is not irritated when we come to ask for help. He never refuses, He never offers excuses, He never argues. He loves us and is anxious to meet our every need. He is generous to us. You can be sure that the begging neighbor would have to pay back whatever he borrowed, but God does not require this of His children. He gives graciously and generously to us, and He keeps on giving.

Does verse 8 teach that we must keep beating on God's door until He answers? Does prayer mean trying to overcome God's unwillingness to act? Of course not! The word translated "importunity" means "shamelessness." I think it applies, not to the man at the door, but to the man in bed. The neighbor was ashamed not to help his friend, for he knew that, if he violated the social code, he would be the target of abuse throughout the whole village. A father, however, meets the needs of his children not to avoid shame, but to express love.

What, then, did Jesus mean when He commanded in verse 9, "Keep on asking . . . keep on seeking . . . keep on knocking . . ."? Is He not encouraging persistence in prayer? Yes, He is; but please note that He immediately ties this admonition to *sonship* in verse 11: "If a son shall ask bread . . ." A son should not come to a father *only when there is a crisis or an emergency*. He should keep in *constant* fellowship with his father, enjoying the father's love and learning the father's will. Then, when there *is* a crisis, he and the father will not be strangers. Persistence in prayer does not mean that we must twist God's arm to get what we want. It means keeping in close communion with the Father, knowing His will, and asking Him to perform His will.

We must never be afraid of answered prayer in the will of God. A loving Father will never give His son anything that will harm him. If a son asks for bread, he will not be given a stone. The Father knows what we need, and He will give us what is right. *Never be afraid to pray and never be afraid of the answer*. It has often been said, "Your Father in heaven loves you too much to harm you, and He is too wise to make a mistake."

We have graduated through three levels in the School of Prayer, and we have learned three lessons: (1) We must pray, (2) we must pray in God's will, and (3) we must pray as children coming to a Father. There is another level.

Graduate School: We Must Pray for the Best Blessings (11:13)

It is not necessary for us as God's children to pray for the Holy Spirit, because He was given to us the moment we trusted Christ (Rom. 8:9; 1 Cor. 6:19–20). When God gave us the Holy Spirit, He gave us all the good things we will ever need for our spiritual walk. The parallel verse in Matthew 7:11 makes this clear: "If ye then, being evil, know how to give good gifts unto your children, how much more shall your Father which is in heaven give good things to them that ask Him?" The good things of the Holy Spirit are the best blessings God has to offer.

It is not wrong to ask God for bread for ourselves. "Give us this day our daily bread" is a legitimate request for the child of God. It is not a sin to ask God to provide material needs, but this is not the highest kind of praying.

Nor is it wrong to ask for bread for others. One of the joys of the Christian life is to see God provide the needs of others because we have helped in praying. The others may not even know that we prayed, but God knows and we know, and He lets us share in the blessing.

I fear that too much of our praying is centered on *things*. If you attend the average prayer meeting, or examine the prayer list of the average church, you will find the emphasis is on the physical and the material. Let me state clearly that it is not wrong to pray for physical healing, or for money needed for the ministry, or for jobs or any other material need. *But we must not stay on that level.* We must graduate into the highest level of praying, asking for the blessings of the Spirit of God that result in Christian character and conduct that glorify the Lord.

Paul prayed for the blessings of the Spirit. His magnificent prayers (Phil. 1:9–11; Eph. 1:15–23; 3:14–21; Col. 1:9–12) are all centered on the blessings of the Spirit of God. He prays about love, discernment, maturity, obedience, faith, power—blessings that only the indwelling Holy Spirit can give us. I am sure that Paul also prayed about bread, physical protection, mercies for travel, and all the other things that seem to play a large part in our own prayers. But Paul went beyond these things and asked God for the good things of the Holy Spirit—Christian character and conduct.

When we understand this graduate level of prayer, we have a better appreciation of the meaning of unanswered prayer. We pray for certain things (money, healing, a job) and God does not answer. It may be that He cannot trust us with these things until our Christian character has grown. No father would give a child a sharp knife or a loaded gun, no matter how much the child begged. No mother would give her little daughter the keys to the family car or the privilege of playing in the medicine chest. God cannot put *things* into our hands until first He prepares our hearts. He uses things as tools to build our Christian character, not as toys to entertain and pamper us.

I read somewhere that the greatest blessing of prayer is not in receiving the answer, but in being the kind of person God can trust with the answer. It is something like an athlete: it is good to win the game, but it is better to be the kind of healthy, coordinated person who can play the game. The excitement of the victory will fade, but the blessing of a strong, healthy body remains. We rejoice at answered prayer, but we should rejoice more that God has brought us to the place spiritually where He can afford to answer our prayers.

The most important part of our lives is the part that only God sees. The hidden life of prayer is the secret of an open life of victory. We must pray, and pray in the will of God. We must pray as children coming to a father. And we must pray for the best blessings of the Holy Spirit.

Have You Met Yourself in This Parable?

1. Do you pray?

2. At what level in the School of Prayer are you right now? Were you ever at a higher level?

3. What needs to be done to reach a higher level?

4. Are you afraid to pray about some things?

5. What blessings of the Holy Spirit have you experienced in your life recently?

6. When God does not answer your prayers, what is your attitude toward Him?

ADDITIONAL NOTE: *The parable of the friend at midnight is similar to the parable of the widow in Luke 18:1–8; and the argument is the same. If a crooked judge finally gives a poor widow what she legally deserves, how much more shall our loving heavenly Father give His children what they need? It is another study in contrasts. Christians are not like that widow, for we are God's children and not strangers to Him. We have open access into His presence, and He has promised to meet every need. We come to a concerned Father, not to a selfish judge. What an encouragement for prayer!*

Luke 16:1–15

And He said also unto His disciples, "There was a certain rich man, which had a steward; and the same was accused unto him that he had wasted his goods. [2]And he called him, and said unto him, 'How is it that I hear this of thee? Give an account of thy stewardship; for thou mayest be no longer steward.' [3]Then the steward said within himself, 'What shall I do? For my lord taketh away from me the stewardship: I cannot dig; to beg I am ashamed. [4]I am resolved what to do, that, when I am put out of the stewardship, they may receive me into their houses.' [5]So he called every one of his lord's debtors unto him, and said unto the first, 'How much owest thou unto my lord?' [6]And he said, 'An hundred measures of oil.' And he said unto him, 'Take thy bill, and sit down quickly, and write fifty.' [7]Then said he to another, 'And how much owest thou?' And he said, 'An hundred measures of wheat.' And he said unto him, 'Take thy bill, and write fourscore.' [8]And the lord commended the unjust steward, because he had done wisely: for the children of this world are in their generation wiser than the children of light. [9]And I say unto you, make to yourselves friends of the mammon of unrighteousness; that, when ye fail, they may receive you into everlasting habitations. [10]He that is faithful in that which is least is faithful also in much: and he that is unjust in the least is unjust also in much. [11]If therefore ye have not been faithful in the unrighteous mammon, who will commit to your trust the true riches? [12]And if ye have not been faithful in that which is another man's, who shall give you that which is your own? [13]No servant can serve two masters: for either he will hate the one, and love the other; or else he will hold to the one, and despise the other. Ye cannot serve God and mammon." [14]And the Pharisees also, who were covetous, heard all these things: and they derided Him. [15]And He said unto them, "Ye are they which justify yourselves before men; but God knoweth your hearts: for that which is highly esteemed among men is abomination in the sight of God."

7
Rude Awakenings
The Parable of the Unjust Steward

A modern businessman can certainly identify with the elements in this parable! Dishonest employees, kick-backs, price-fixing—they have always been a part of business and probably always will be. The amazing thing is that Christ used these things to teach important spiritual lessons.

He told this parable to His disciples, but the Pharisees were listening (v. 14). The Lord wanted to teach two important lessons: (1) the wise use of opportunities, and (2) the danger of covetousness. If believers would make as wise decisions as business-men do—but with the right motives—they would accomplish more for the kingdom of God. When this steward discovered he was facing a crisis (the boss was auditing the books), and would certainly lose his position, he made the wisest use of the situation and prepared for the future.

A crisis does not make a man but it shows what a man is made of. The Lord Jesus did not commend this steward for his unethical actions. He commended him for his wise use of his opportunities: "The children of this world are in their generation wiser than the children of light" (v. 8). They are not wiser when it comes to spiritual things, and their wisdom extends only to their generation and not to eternity. But we can learn from this dishonest employee how to make the most of our opportunities.

This steward was able to make the most of his situation because he responded properly to the *insights* that came to him in the crisis. For the first time in his life, he could see things clearly.

He Saw Himself

It is amazing how we can go along in life and never really see ourselves. A famous psychologist wrote, "Nothing, indeed, is so likely to shock us at first as the manifest revelation of ourselves." Peter was sure he could never deny the Lord. Few of us enjoy looking at the unretouched proofs from our latest photograph.

When the crisis came, this man suddenly realized that *he was a steward.* He owned nothing but had the privilege of managing everything for his master. He was paid by his master and was expected to be honest and faithful. Like Joseph in Potiphar's house, this man had his master's wealth in his control and was supposed to manage it for his master's good.

Does it come as a shock to you that *you do not own anything?* You may *possess* many things, but you do not own them. God owns them. He is the Master and we are the stewards. He gives us the privilege of using His vast wealth, and He gives us the responsibility of using it faithfully. Paul wrote, "Moreover it is required in stewards, that a man be found faithful" (1 Cor. 4:2). God wants us to *employ* His wealth for the advancement of His kingdom, and He wants us to *enjoy* His wealth and be thankful (1 Tim. 6:17–19).

In what respects are Christians "stewards"? Certainly we are stewards of *our time*: "See then that ye walk circumspectly [carefully], not as fools, but as wise, redeeming the time [buying up the opportunity], because the days are evil" (Eph. 5:15–16). It is as much a sin to waste time as it is to waste money or food. God gives each of us 24 hours a day, and we must invest that time wisely to the glory of God. If your doctor told you, "You have only six months to live," you would suddenly awaken to the fact that time is precious and must not be squandered.

We are also stewards of *our gifts and abilities*: "As every man hath received the gift, even so minister the same one to another, as good stewards of the manifold grace of God" (1 Peter 4:10). God in His grace has given each of His children spiritual gifts, and natural abilities; and these should be used to build His church. How tragic it is that churches and mission boards cannot find the dedicated talent they need to win souls and extend God's work!

A friend of mine experienced a rude awakening when she almost died. It was a touch-and-go situation, but the Lord pulled her through. She had always been a devoted Christian and busy in His service, but after her recovery, she was busier than ever.

"I told the Lord I would do *anything* He asked me to do, so long as He would help me do it," she explained. "I wasn't bargaining with Him for my life. I was willing for Him to take me Home. But I just wanted Him to know that I was available." She is one of the most encouraging Christians I know.

You and I are also *stewards of the Gospel*: "But as we were allowed of God to be put in trust with the Gospel . . ." (1 Thes. 2:4). This is the greatest treasure God has put into our hands. It is our responsibility to guard this message and to share it with others (2 Tim. 1:13–14; 2:2). It is important that the church "buy up the opportunity" and share the good news of salvation with as many people as possible. When the president announced diplomatic recognition of mainland China, the American business community immediately negotiated to establish offices in China! They knew how to be ready for open doors.

The emphasis in the parable is on the stewardship of *material possessions*. We commonly think of stewardship as a philosophy of giving, how a person should calculate tithes and offerings. But this is a mistaken idea. Stewardship has to do with how a believer uses *everything* he possesses, and not just his money. We are to be good stewards in the way we use our car, our tools, our house, our clothing—everything that we have. Stewardship does not mean giving 10 percent to God and then wasting the remaining 90 percent. It means using the 100 percent wholly for the Lord as He directs.

He Saw Life

Keep in mind that the parable of the unjust steward was given just after the famous parable of the prodigal (wasteful) son (Luke 15). When you put the two parables together, and look at the three persons involved (the prodigal, the elder brother, and the steward), you can see three different philosophies of life.

The prodigal's philosophy was to *waste life*. He "wasted his substance with riotous living" (Luke 15:13). He lived for the moment and had no thought for the future.

The elder brother simply *spent his life*. He was a drudge. He obeyed his father's will but had no enjoyment in what he was doing. He was always hoping that the future would be better, that perhaps he might be able to "make merry" with his friends (Luke 15:29). The elder brother represents many honest, hard-working people that we know, who are trusting that the future will be better than the present.

The steward learned there was a third philosophy, apart from *wasting* life and *spending* life. He could *invest* his life. Instead of destroying his future by living only for the present (like the prodigal), or destroying his present by hoping for the future (like the elder brother), he could *live the present in the light of the future.* The steward used his present opportunities to assure himself a secure future. Jesus did not approve of the way he did it, but He commended him for the fact that he did it.

When the crisis came and the master asked to see the books, the steward saw life in a new light. He realized that he had been wasting his life and living a lie. He called his master "Master," but in reality *money* was his master. He was even willing to cheat to get money! Money is a marvelous servant, but a terrible master. Paul warned, "For the love of money is a root of all sorts of evil" (1 Tim. 6:10, NASB).

Not only was the steward living for the wrong master, but he was also living for the wrong motive. He was living to please himself and not to please his master. He robbed his master to please himself, but actually he was robbing himself. His sins caught up with him.

I remember waking up in an intensive care ward of a hospital after a serious auto accident in which a drunken driver hit my car at the speed of 80 miles per hour. The hospital chaplain had told my wife that I would never make it through the night. Hundreds of God's people were praying and God graciously spared my life. When they wheeled me out of that intensive care ward a week later and moved me to my own room, you can be sure I had a new appreciation of life! I realized as never before that life is a wonderful series of opportunities to serve God and do His will, and that anything else is not worth living for. You can be sure too that I had rearranged priorities in my life, determining with God's help to make the most of every opportunity He might give me.

If you discovered that today was the last day of your life, how much rearranging would you have to do?

He Saw His Master

We have no reason to believe that the master was a hard man or a crooked businessman. When he heard that the steward had been cheating him, he immediately called for the books. He could have put the steward in jail, but instead, he only fired him. Between the time he was fired, and the time the news got out, the steward called in his master's tenants and lowered that year's rent. Had they known he was fired, they would never have done business with him. In this way, the steward accomplished two things: (1) he made some friends for the future, and (2) he proved that he was a shrewd manager, capable of acting in a crisis.

Up to the time of the crisis, the steward had considered his master a soft touch, a distant person about whom he did not have to worry. But when the order came to bring in the books for auditing, the steward suddenly realized that he was doing business with a real person who meant business. He had forgotten that stewardship involves not only responsibility and privilege, but it also involves *accountability*. It was great fun to write checks and pad his own wallet, but then the day of reckoning arrived.

Christians have a tendency to forget that one day an account must be given to the Lord. "For we must all appear before the judgment seat of Christ; that every one may receive the things done in his body, according to that he hath done, whether it be good or bad" (2 Cor. 5:10).

The Bible makes it clear that Christians will not be judged for their sins. These are remembered against them no more (Heb. 10:17), and they can never be condemned for them (John 5:24; Rom. 8:1). It is *works* that will be judged, and this judgment will determine the rewards Christians shall receive (1 Cor. 3:11–15).

If Christians really believe they will one day give an accounting to God, this conviction will show up in their lives—in their use of time, talents, and treasures.

The steward made some radical changes in his life when he realized he was going to face his master and give account. He started using present opportunities for future blessings. He started living for people and not for things, for investment and not for mere enjoyment.

Jesus made the application very clear: "And I say unto you, make to yourselves friends [by means] of the mammon of unrighteousness [material goods, money]; that, when ye fail, they [your friends] may receive you into everlasting habitations" (v. 9). If we use our material possessions wisely today, we will enjoy them more, *and* we will have friends in heaven who came to know Christ because we were faithful stewards.

We get the idea that only wealthy people should be good stewards. After all, middle- and lower-income people do not have as much to give. But the issue is not the portion—it's the *proportion*. Whether we are rich or poor, or in between, we can dedicate *all that we have* to winning souls and serving God's people.

Jesus Christ is not a hard master. His yoke is easy

and His burden is light. It would be good to remind ourselves that Jesus Christ will one day sit on His judgment seat and ask each of us for an accounting of our stewardship.

He Saw Possessions

Before the crisis came, the steward lived for things. He stole from his master in order to enjoy life. But then he was shocked into realizing that things are not an end in themselves. Rather, they are a means to an end. That realization changed his life.

Of itself, money is useless. You cannot eat it, it will not heal you, and it would take a great deal of it to keep you warm. Money is a medium of exchange. Simply to amass money is no guarantee of happiness. In fact, the Bible teaches that the desire to amass money is the cause of a great deal of unhappiness. "My power is as great as the power of money," wrote Karl Marx, one of the architects of Communism. Yet Jesus Christ was poor and exercised a power that still changes lives.

Henry Fielding, the novelist, wrote, "If you make money your god, it will plague you like the devil." How much better to let God be the Lord of our possessions! Perhaps you heard about the wealthy man who prayed at family devotions that God would meet the needs of a number of missionary friends. After he had said "Amen," his little son said: "Dad, if I had your checkbook, I could answer your prayers for you!"

The steward discovered that wealth was only a means to an end—a means of helping others and investing in the future. To be sure, we do not approve of the way he did it but we do approve of his change of heart. He saw possessions in a new light and began to use them in a new way.

He Saw His Friends
The steward gained a whole new outlook on his friends. Up to the time of the audit, he had used his friends to rob his master and line his own pocket. Now he realized that his friends could be *friends*. They could welcome him into their homes when he was out of a job. He could help them and they could help him.

Of course, Jesus is not suggesting that we get our friends involved in some crooked deal so we can blackmail them into helping us. He is reminding us that we must *use our opportunities to make friends for heaven* so that when life ends they will receive us into "everlasting habitations" (v. 9).

Jesus closed the lesson by emphasizing the importance of *faithfulness* (vv. 10–13). He pointed out that Christians have two kinds of wealth, namely, material and spiritual.

Verses 10–12 may be outlined like this:

The material	The spiritual
Mammon	God
that which is least	much
unrighteous mammon	true riches
that which is another's	that which is your own

We commonly think that the person who handles a great deal of wealth will naturally be careful about small amounts, but this is not always true. In fact, if you can trust a man with a small amount, and he proves faithful, you can trust him with a larger amount. This explains why church officers should be proved in lesser ministries before being given great spiritual responsibilities (1 Tim. 3:10).

But there is another truth here: the person who is unfaithful with material wealth cannot be trusted with spiritual wealth. There is a definite relationship between the way a Christian uses money and the way he ministers the truths of God's Word. It is tragic when so-called evangelical ministries go bankrupt or get into serious financial trouble because of misman-agement. I believe that Christians should be as fundamental in their financial policies as they are in their doctrinal statements.

What is it that tempts people into unfaithfulness and dishonesty? The Lord stated that they want the praises of men instead of the approval of God (Luke 16:15). These words of Jesus are really convicting: "That which is highly esteemed among men is abomination in the sight of God." Does this mean that it is a sin for a Christian to be rich? Of course not! Abraham and Job were wealthy men, yet God approved of them. But it is a sin for a Christian to *measure his worth* by riches. This explains why the Pharisees (who overheard the parable) laughed at Jesus. They were covetous of riches and even used their religion to acquire riches from innocent people (Matt. 23:14–22).

I wonder what our Lord would say about the present-day philosophy that says, "If you are a dedicated Christian, God will give you the very best! There is no reason why you shouldn't live in the best house, drive the best car, and make the best salary." Such blessings are not necessarily a proof of dedica-tion and devotion. Throughout Bible history and church history many outstanding people were poor.

Money is a marvelous servant, but a terrible master. A person should use what he has in Christ's service. He should not waste his life or merely spend it. He should invest his life by being faithful.

Have You Met Yourself in This Parable?

1. Which philosophy of life would you hold to: the prodigal's, the elder brother's, or the steward's? Why?

2. Are you as wise in your spiritual decisions as you are in your financial and business decisions?

3. Suppose some local business operated the same way as your local church. How successful would they be?

4. When the Lord provides you with some extra money, what is your *first* response?

5. Are you practicing giving, tithing, or stewardship?

6. Can you honestly say you are faithful in the little things?

7. Are you using your material wealth to impress people or to serve the Lord?

Luke 14:1–24

And it came to pass, as He went into the house of one of the chief Pharisees to eat bread on the Sabbath Day, that they watched Him. [2]And, behold, there was a certain man before Him which had the dropsy. [3]And Jesus answering spake unto the lawyers and Pharisees, saying, "Is it lawful to heal on the Sabbath Day?" [4]And they held their peace. And He took him, and healed him, and let him go; [5]and answered them, saying, "Which of you shall have an ass or an ox fallen into a pit, and will not straightway pull him out on the Sabbath Day?" [6]And they could not answer Him again to these things. [7]And He put forth a parable to those which were bidden, when he marked how they chose out the chief rooms; saying unto them, [8]"when thou art bidden of any man to a wedding, sit not down in the highest room; lest a more honorable man than thou be bidden of him; [9]and he that bade thee and him come and say to thee, 'Give this man place;' and thou begin with shame to take the lowest room. [10]But when thou art bidden, go and sit down in the lowest room; that when he that bade thee cometh, he may say unto thee, 'Friend, go up higher:' then shalt thou have worship in the presence of them that sit at meat with thee. [11]For whosoever exalteth himself shall be abased; and he that humbleth himself shall be exalted." [12]Then said He also to him that bade him, "When thou makest a dinner or a supper, call not thy friends, nor thy brethren, neither thy kinsman, nor thy rich neighbors; lest they also bid thee again, and a recompense be made thee. [13]But when thou makest a feast, call the poor, the maimed, the lame, the blind: [14]and thou shalt be blessed; for they cannot recompense thee; for thou shalt be recompensed at the resurrection of the just." [15]And when one of them that sit at meat with Him heard these things, he said unto Him, "Blessed is he that shall eat bread in the kingdom of God." [16]Then said He unto him, "A certain man made a great supper, and bade many: [17]and sent his servant at supper time to say to them that were bidden, 'Come; for all things are now ready.' [18]And they all with one consent began to make excuse. The first said unto him, 'I have bought a piece of ground, and I must needs go and see it: I pray thee have me excused.' [19]And another said, 'I have bought five yoke of oxen, and I go to prove them: I pray thee have me excused.'

[20]And another said, 'I have married a wife, and therefore I cannot come.' [21]So that servant came, and showed his lord these things. Then the master of the house being angry said to his servant, 'Go out quickly into the streets and lanes of the city, and bring in hither the poor, and the maimed, and the halt, and the blind.' [22]And the servant said, 'Lord it is done as thou hast commanded, and yet there is room.' [23]And the lord said unto the servant, 'Go out into the highways and hedges, and compel them to come in, that my house may be filled. [24]For I say unto you, that none of those men which were bidden shall taste of my supper.' "

8
Table Talk
The Parable of the Great Supper

How many times have you seen this motto hanging on the wall in a Christian home?—"Jesus Christ is the Head of this home, the silent Listener to every conversation, the unseen Guest at every meal."

These are worthy sentiments and the consciousness of these truths would make us easier to live with at home. But I wonder how many of us would *really* want Jesus Christ at our table? He can be a very dangerous Guest! A Pharisee discovered that fact when he invited the Lord to his home for a Sabbath breakfast. The Lord's table talk was anything but idle conversation. During that meal, Jesus told several parables (climaxing with the parable of the great supper), and in these parables He taught several important lessons.

A Lesson in Sympathy (14:1–6)

As Jesus and the other guests were gathering, a man with dropsy stood immediately in front of Jesus, as if to attract attention. We are not sure whether the man wandered in off the street or whether the Lord's enemies planted him there to trap Him. The rabbis and lawyers made a big case out of the question, "Is it lawful to heal on the Sabbath?" If Jesus did not heal the man, He was showing unconcern and lack of compassion, but if He did heal the man, He was violating the Sabbath. What would He do?

It is sad to think these religious leaders may have been using this afflicted man as a tool to fulfill their evil purposes. They had no real concern for the man. They were openly exposing his handicap and deliberately creating a problem for him and he could do nothing about it.

Yet in our own modern civilization are there not times when we exploit people and use their weaknesses to our advantage? Jesus never did that. In this case, He took the man, healed him, and let him go. And then He defended His actions with a parable about the ox (or "son" in some versions) and donkey in the well. With the parable, Jesus was asking "Should you treat your animals better than I treat a man made in God's image?" In other words, "If the Sabbath is a holy day, then let it be filled with holy deeds!"

Many people *do* treat their pets better than they treat the members of their own families. Brothers and sisters will fight each other, using all kinds of abusive language, but hug and kiss the family dog or cat and treat it like a king or queen. Sad to say, adults will do the same things. More money is spent on dog food in the United States than on foreign missions. I am not suggesting that the dogs go hungry, but I am concerned that people stop treating animals like people and people like animals.

A Lesson in Humility (14:7–11)

While He was healing the man, Jesus had watched the guests assemble and fight for the best seats. The Pharisees always wanted the best seats at the feasts (Matt. 23:6) and their guests followed their bad example. We laugh at this, but the same mad scramble goes on today. There are more status seekers and pyramid climbers in churches and other Christian organizations than we care to admit. The competition can be strong as Christians argue over who has the greatest church, the biggest Sunday School, or the most sacrificial missionary program.

This mad scramble for the top seats only shows how false is our view of success. As if *where* a man sits can change the man! "Try not to become a man of success," said Albert Einstein, "but rather try to become a man of value." Paul sat in a prison while Nero sat on the throne of the Roman Empire, yet no one doubts who was the better man. The cream may rise to the top in milk, but often the flotsam and jetsam rises to the top on the sea of life.

In order to get the best seats, these status seekers had to climb over other people, using them like rungs on a ladder just to achieve what they thought was success. In His parable, Jesus pointed out the pitfalls in this philosophy of life. To begin with, *we* are not in charge of the seating, the host is. "But God is the Judge; He puts down one, and exalts another" (Ps. 75:7, NASB). Any status we achieve by our own push is temporary, and it could turn out to be very embarrassing.

It is one thing to have ambition, but quite another thing to be selfishly ambitious for position and power. The man with true ambition will prepare himself, be faithful in his work, and watch for God-given opportunities for growth and advancement. He knows there are no successful shortcuts to the top. The ambitious man is so concerned with the end he is not careful about the means to the end, and he will use any means, fair or foul, to get to the top.

A successful insurance man I know resigned his top position to start at the bottom in a different company.

He explained his decision to me as we sat in his office. "I got to the top by bluffing. I didn't really learn the business as I should. I had a successful business, but I was not a successful person. My character suffered. Now I'm starting all over at the bottom, and it's terrific what the Lord is doing in me!"

A person's worth is not based on position, a title on the door, or the applause of people, but on Christian character and his relationship to God.

A Lesson in Generosity (14:12–14)

Having taught the proud guests a lesson, Jesus then turned to the host and tried to help him. The Lord noticed that the Pharisee had invited as guests only the people who were important, influential, and rich. These guests probably would, in turn, invite the host to their houses, and on and on it would go. These people really were not hungry and they did not need the meal.

Christ was not opposing hospitality or showing hospitality to those who can repay us. The tense of the Greek verb in verse 12 helps us understand His statement: "When you give a luncheon or a dinner, do not *always keep inviting* your friends" (literal translation). In other words, do not get into the habit of entertaining only those who entertain you.

Before we criticize this Pharisee, let's examine our own social life to see whether or not we may belong to a Christian clique or an evangelical mutual admiration society. There is nothing wrong with enjoying the fellowship of good friends, but we are sinning if we do this exclusively. It is difficult for visitors, and even new church members, to break into the exclusive clubs that form in almost every local church. Shame on those saintly social climbers who want to be seen with what they think are the best people.

Jesus taught us to live to serve others and to get our reward from God alone. A pastor friend of mine, now with the Lord, often reminded me, "You can't get your reward twice. You will get it either from men today or the Lord tomorrow." Of course, there is an inner joy and enrichment when we obey the Lord and share with those less fortunate than we are. But there is also an eternal reward from the Lord if we have served Him and our motives have been pure.

Christian hospitality is an exciting ministry. "Being given to hospitality" (Rom. 12:13) is a mark of a Christian. Peter admonished believers who were going through suffering, "Use hospitality one to another without grudging" (1 Peter 4:9). And the writer to the Hebrews wrote, "Be not forgetful to entertain strangers. For thereby some have entertained angels unawares" (Heb. 13:2). No matter what may be your views on the second coming of Christ, you must admit that the Lord emphasized practical hospitality (see Matt. 25:31ff).

The Lord gave three practical lessons on sympathy, humility, and generosity. At that point one of the guests (probably under conviction) thought he would make a spiritual remark, so he shouted, "Blessed is he that shall eat bread in the kingdom of God" (Luke 14:15). This remark led Jesus to give the climactic parable of the meal, the parable of the great supper.

A Lesson in Opportunity (14:15–24)

"How do you even know you will enter the kingdom of God?" Jesus was saying to the man who spoke. "If you don't use the opportunities you have right now, you may find the door shut in your face!" It is not enough to make pious speeches. You must respond to God's invitation.

The parable of the great supper has three scenes.

1. Preparation—*"All things are now ready"* *(14:17)*. It is interesting that Christ compares salvation to a feast. To look at many believers, you would think that the Christian life was a fast, a funeral, or a famine! God is like a next-door neighbor who spreads a great feast on the table. He knows that, as lost sinners, people are hungry and thirsty and ready to die. The water of this world does not satisfy (John 4:13–14), and the bread that people buy at a dear price can never meet their needs (Isa. 55:1–2).

Of the many pictures of salvation in the Bible the feast certainly is one of the most meaningful. I have never searched for a lost sheep or delivered a baby, but I have sat down at a good dinner and enjoyed the food. You and I can identify with this kind of illustration!

Salvation, like food at a meal, must be received *within*. A hungry guest could sit at the table and admire the food, yet starve to death. Jesus Christ is the Bread of Life, and He must be received *within* before He can save us (John 6:48–51). Our physical food only *sustains* life, but the Bread of Life *imparts* life to the dead sinner.

When you think of a feast, you also think of *joy*. Those who have received Jesus Christ into their lives have experienced the "good tidings of great joy" that belong to salvation (Luke 2:10).

The main point, however, is this: the feast is prepared by God, and sinners need do nothing but "come and dine." Jesus called it a "great supper" because it was planned and executed out of a great love, it met a great need, and it cost a great price. Occasionally, my wife comes home from grocery shopping mumbling to herself, "Such prices!" But think of the price God paid to spread the table with salvation's supper.

Two little words stand out in verse 17: *all* and *now*. God has done *all* that needed to be done to save lost sinners. Christ finished the work of redemption on the cross. The table is spread with all that we need: forgiveness, cleansing, peace, joy, and much more. And it is *now* ready. Paul wrote, "Behold, now is the accepted time; behold, now is the day of salvation" (2 Cor. 6:2). The sign outside the door of the dining hall reads: "No waiting!" It is all ready now.

2. *Invitation—"Come" (14:17)*. God has prepared salvation for a lost world and He sends His servants out to invite people to come in. God's desire is to fill His house. Of course, this was not the first invitation that had gone out, for it was customary among middle eastern people to invite the guests in advance, and then to send a second invitation at the time of the feast.

"Come" is certainly one of the great words of the Gospel. Religion tells the sinner to "do" or "go" (perhaps on a pilgrimage), or "pay" or "hope," but Christ says to all, "Come!" Someone has said that C is for children, O is for older people, M is for middle-aged people, and E is for everybody. Nobody is left out of God's gracious invitation. The Apostle John was told "And the Spirit and the bride say, 'Come.' And let the one who hears say, 'Come.' And let the one who is thirsty come; let the one who wishes take the water of life without cost" (Rev. 22:17, NASB).

"Come" indicates the *simplicity* of salvation. All a person need do is take that step of faith and trust Christ. It also announces the *availability* of salvation. The door is open and the feast has been spread. "Come" also suggests the *responsibility* a person has to act on God's gracious invitation. To be sure, salvation begins with God, but God's invitation is addressed to a person's mind, heart, and will. There is no conflict between divine sovereignty and human responsibility, though with our limited vision we cannot see where they meet.

You would expect *everybody* to respond enthusiastically and come to the feast. But this was not the case. Those invited began to make excuses. Any man who buys a piece of property *before* he looks at it is a fool, and so is the man who purchases 10 oxen without first proving them (that would be like buying a car you never drove). The man who was newly married could have brought his bride with him.

These people did not reject the invitation because they were involved in *bad* activities. There is nothing essentially wrong with real estate, plowing, or enjoying your home. These people were rejecting *the best* and settling for *second-best*. Most of the people who reject God's gracious invitation today are not involved in gross iniquities. They are just too involved in the everyday affairs of life and too busy to think seriously about what they are doing.

If I were to list the causes behind these excuses, I would say: (1) they did not know their own deep needs, (2) they could not realize what they were missing, (3) they had no respect for the one who invited them, and (4) they really expected to get a second chance. Only the newly-wed said, "I cannot come." The others said, "Please have me excused." That really means, "I'm not coming now, but I may come if you invite me again." But they never had that second opportunity. This leads to the third scene in the parable.

3. *Condemnation (14:21–24).* The host became angry. We do not often think about the anger of God, because there is so much emphasis on the love of God, but God does get angry. After all, He had planned the supper and He had paid the price. The

guests were really insulting Him, for in middle eastern countries, to turn down an invitation was a serious thing. It could even lead to war if the rejected invitation came from a leader.

People who refuse God's loving invitation have no respect for the Lord. Paul said, "There is no fear of God before their eyes" (Rom. 3:18). God's invitation is not *a suggestion*, but *a command*. God "commandeth all men everywhere to repent" (Acts 17:30). To reject His invitation is to disobey His will.

How did the host show his anger? He sent the servant to invite other guests. He did not plead with the guests who had insulted him, he simply found others to take their place. The servant scoured the streets and lanes of the city and brought in "the poor and crippled and blind and lame" (Luke 14:21, NASB). Since there was still room, the servant left the city and went into the country where the pilgrims walked the highways and the vagrants slept in the hedgerows. These people responded and filled the house.

Why did these outsiders accept the invitation while the insiders refused it? *They knew their need.* They were lonely, hungry, thirsty, and ready to die. Furthermore, they were not welcome anywhere else, for who is likely to invite that kind of a crowd to a feast? Only the Lord welcomes people nobody else wants.

These rejected people would not make excuses or postpone accepting the invitation. When they first heard the invitation, they undoubtedly said, "This is too good to be true!" But they believed the message, came to the feast, and discovered they were welcome. The poor would not be out buying real estate and the crippled were not likely to be proving oxen.

It seems the Lord was warning the Jewish people that, if they rejected Him, God would extend the invitation to the Gentiles—and this is just what He did. But there is a personal lesson here: *no one dare trifle with the Gospel invitation*, for the next thing the host did was *close the door*. He said, "None of those men which were bidden shall taste of my supper" (v. 24). No wonder the prophet warns, "Seek ye the Lord while He may be found, call ye upon Him while He is near" (Isa. 55:6). If any of the original guests decided to come to the feast, he discovered that the door was shut and his opportunity gone.

Have You Met Yourself in This Parable?

1. Which of the four lessons do you think is most needed in your life just now: sympathy, humility, generosity, or opportunity?

2. Would you consider yourself a status seeker?

3. What have you done personally to make the newcomer feel welcome to your church or Bible study group?

4. Do you enjoy serving God anonymously so that nobody can pay you back?

5. God wants His house filled. What are you doing to see His desires fulfilled?

6. If you have never trusted Christ, what excuses are you giving? Do you really think the Lord will accept them?

Luke 11:14–26

[14]"And He was casting out a devil, and it was dumb. And it came to pass, when the devil was gone out, the dumb spake; and the people wondered. [15]But some of them said, "He casteth out devils through Beelzebub the chief of the devils." [16]And others, tempting Him, sought of Him a sign from heaven. [17]But He, knowing their thoughts, said unto them, "Every kingdom divided against itself is brought to desolation; and a house divided against a house falleth. [18]If Satan also be divided against himself, how shall his kingdom stand? Because ye say that I cast out devils through Beelzebub. [19]And if I by Beelzebub cast out devils, by whom do your sons cast them out? Therefore shall they be your judges. [20]But if I with the finger of God cast out devils, no doubt the kingdom of God is come upon you. [21]When a strong man armed keepeth his palace, his goods are in peace: [22]but when a stronger than he shall come upon him, and overcome him, he taketh from him all his armor wherein he trusted, and divideth his spoils. [23]He that is not with Me is against Me: and he that gathereth not with Me scattereth. [24]When the unclean spirit is gone out of a man, he walketh through dry places, seeking rest; and finding none, he saith 'I will return unto my house whence I came out.' [25]And when he cometh, he findeth it swept and garnished. [26]Then goeth he, and taketh to him seven other spirits more wicked than himself; and they enter in, and dwell there: and the last state of that man is worse than the first."

9
Battle Stations
The Parable of the Strong Man

When congregations at Christmastime sing "Peace on earth and mercy mild," they are expressing only one aspect of the Christmas story. Our Lord's birth at Bethlehem involved *war* as well as peace. It was part of an agelong conflict between God and Satan, a war that was declared in Genesis 3:15. You and I are not merely spectators—we must be participants. This is one war in which it is impossible to be neutral. We are either with Him or against Him.

Consider the stages in Christ's war against Satan.

Christ Invaded Satan's Territory
When the religious leaders accused Christ of casting out demons by the power of Satan, He refuted their statement with two arguments. First, He pointed out that if Satan is fighting against himself, that is the end of his kingdom. Their statement was *illogical*, for no enemy fights against himself. But He also pointed out that their statement was *inconsistent*, for this would mean that "their sons" (other Jewish exorcists) were also casting out demons in the power of Satan. Of course, the scribes were not prepared to admit that.

Jesus' reply reveals that Satan has a kingdom and a house. This present world system is Satan's kingdom.

The Bible uses the word *world* in several different senses. There is the world of *people*: "God so loved the world" (John 3:16). There is also the world of *matter*: "God, who made the world and all things in it" (Acts 17:24, NASB). But there is also a *world system* behind the visible world that we see, and it is this world that Satan rules. "Now is the judgment of this world; now shall the prince of this world be cast out" (John 12:31). Jesus called Satan "the prince of this world" (John 14:30 and 16:11).

This does not mean that Satan runs the material world, for this is in God's hands (read Psalms 147 and 148), but it does mean that Satan rules in the lives of people who have never been born again. Paul called Satan "the prince of the power of the air, the spirit that now worketh in the children of disobedience" (Eph. 2:2). The Apostle John wrote, "We know that we are of God, and the whole world lies in the power of [literally, "in the lap of"] the wicked one" (1 John 5:19).

Satan not only controls individuals, but he has an evil influence over nations. Daniel 10:13 names "the prince of the kingdom of Persia" as an adversary of God, one who tried to keep God from answering Daniel's prayer. World history is not simply a record of man's politics, it is also a record of the battle going on in the spirit realm between God and Satan.

Did Satan know that Christ was one day going to come and invade his kingdom? Of course! God's promise of a Redeemer in Genesis 3:15 was proof enough. Satan did all he could to keep the Saviour from being born. He incited Cain to kill Abel so that God had to continue the messianic line through Seth. The mixing of the godly and ungodly in Genesis 6 (some take this to be an invasion of the evil angels) was another satanic device to hinder the coming of

the Messiah. Every attack on Israel in the Old
Testament, such as that of Haman in the Book of
Esther, was an attempt to wipe out God's people and
the messianic hope.

When Jesus was born, Satan tried to kill him
(Matt. 2:16–23). Throughout our Lord's earthly ministry, His enemies repeatedly tried to arrest Him and
even slay Him. Satan entered Judas (John 13:27), who
then sold Jesus to His enemies. But the Cross was not
Satan's victory, *it was Satan's defeat* (Col. 1:13–14;
2:14–15).

It is important to note that, when Jesus took upon
Him a human body, He *permanently* became a part of
the battle on earth. And since His children are united
to Him through the Spirit, He is able to empower
them in their battle against Satan.

We must be careful not to press a parable too far,
for a parable is given to illustrate doctrine, not to
declare it. But the fact that Christ talked about Satan's
"house" (vv. 17, 24) and his "palace" (v. 21) suggests to
me that there is more here than just the scenery of a
play. Certainly, Satan's "house" must be the body of
the person who is being used by Satan to accomplish
his evil deeds. The Greek word translated "palace"
can also be translated "the court of a prince." It is
used this way in some of the papyruses.

The picture given in this parable is that of Jesus
Christ invading Satan's kingdom (the world system),
coming right to his court, and setting free the people
Satan had been guarding. This was the first stage in
our Lord's war against the devil.

Christ Overcame Satan's Power

Satan is pictured as "a strong man armed" (v. 21). J. B.
Phillips, a noted British scholar, translated this
phrase: "a strong man armed to the teeth." Satan does

all he can to protect his kingdom from the Lord's attacks. Never minimize the power and anger of Satan. He is a strong being with great power to do evil.

In verse 15, Satan is called "Beelzebub, the chief of the devils." One of the heathen gods in the Old Testament is Baalzebub (2 Kings 1:2, 6, 16). That name means "Baal, the prince." Beelzebub (or Beelzebul) is variously translated "lord of the height, lord of the flies, lord of the dung." But many students think it means "lord of the dwelling." This fits right in with the picture we have in this parable of Satan guarding his kingdom and house.

Each name that Satan wears teaches us something about his personality and his work. The name Satan means "adversary" (1 Peter 5:8). Devil means "a slanderer." (There is, of course, only one devil but there are many demons and Satan is their prince.) Satan slanders God's people and accuses them (Rev. 12:7–11). He is pictured as a dragon (Rev. 12:7), a lion (1 Peter 5:8), and a serpent (2 Cor. 11:3). While Christ is at work in this world seeking to "gather," Satan is hard at work "scattering" (see v. 23). Christ puts things together, but Satan tears things apart.

Christ met Satan in the wilderness and overcame his every temptation (Matt. 4:1–11). That was the beginning of the victory. During His ministry on earth, Christ overcame Satan's power by healing the diseased, releasing the demon–posessed, and even by raising the dead. Jesus' greatest victory was on the cross, where the "prince of this world" was "cast out" (John 12:31–33). Even though that "hour" belonged to "the power of darkness" (Luke 22:53), Christ won the battle and came forth in resurrection glory. He is now seated in heaven "far above all principality, and power, and might" (Eph. 1:21).

Christ Destroyed Satan's Weapons

What are some of the weapons Satan uses to keep his kingdom under subjection?

1. Pride (1 Tim. 3:6). Pride turned Lucifer the angel into Satan the adversary. He was not content to be a creature, worshiping God, he wanted to be God and be worshiped by the other creatures. (Read Isa. 14:12–15.) Satan even asked Jesus Christ to bow down and worship him (Matt. 4:9).

In every aspect of His life on earth, Jesus rebuked pride. He was born in a humble village and laid in a manger. He willingly laid aside His own glory and independence to come to earth as a servant (Phil. 2:5–11). Lucifer the creature wanted to become the Creator, while Jesus the Creator willingly became a creature. Lucifer said, "I will," but Jesus said, "Not My will, but Thine, be done" (Luke 22:42).

2. Fear (Heb. 2:14–15). Fear is said to be one of the strongest emotions in human life. Certainly, there is a right kind of fear, including the fear of the Lord, but Satan uses a fear that leads to bondage and suffering. The fear of death is one of his chief weapons. No doubt this fear motivates much of the pagan superstitious religion in the world today. It is a good thing to have a healthy fear of death, otherwise you would not live very long. But a superstitious fear that cripples the mind and heart is a weapon of Satan to control and destroy a person.

Jesus Christ has abolished death (2 Tim. 1:10). *Abolished* means "to make inactive, to render useless." Death is still on the scene, of course, but death does not frighten the Christian because Jesus has defused death and it cannot hurt us. The fear of death should not be a problem to the Christian, so Satan cannot use that as a weapon to fight him.

In His life and ministry, Jesus sought to take away

fear. "For God hath not given us the spirit of fear; but of power, and of love, and of a sound mind" (2 Tim. 1:7). Fear and faith cannot live too long in the same heart. As we trust Christ, we can face life unafraid.

3. *Lies (John 8:44).* Satan is a liar and the father of lies. Jesus came to bear witness of the truth (John 18:37). By the way He lived, and by what He taught, Jesus exposed Satan's lies and revealed God's truth.

It is important to note that Satan's lies are often religious lies. He masquerades as an angel of light (2 Cor. 11:13–15) and sends his false apostles to lead people astray. Satan is even able to twist Scripture to lead people away from God's truth and into his deception. Every false cult is based on some misinterpretation of God's Word, and most false cults claim to submit to the authority of the Bible.

The Holy Spirit works in men's lives through truth, but Satan works in men's lives through *lies*. Once you believe a lie, you are open to the working of Satan. As Christians, we must test our thought life by Philippians 4:8, and note that the first test is "Whatsoever things are true . . . "

The entrance of God's Word gives light (Ps. 119:130), but the entrance of Satan's lies produces darkness (2 Cor. 4:4). Satan blinds men's minds, but Christ brightens men's minds. It all depends on what you believe.

When Christ came to earth, He found God's wonderful truth buried under centuries of human tradition. This religious tradition had robbed people of the freedom of truth and had led them into the bondage of lies. One of the first things Jesus had to do was to set God's Word free from man's tradition, and it was this ministry that brought Him into conflict with the Pharisees and scribes.

Christ deliberately healed on the Sabbath Day so

He could call attention to the abuses the religious leaders had foisted upon the people. He and His disciples did not always practice the ceremonial washings, and this gave Jesus the opportunity to point out how the traditionalists had robbed God's Word of its power (Mark 7:1ff). Of all lies, religious lies are the most dangerous for they can result in the eternal condemnation of the human soul.

The test of all teaching is the Word of God. Isaiah wrote, "To the law and to the testimony: if they speak not according to this word, it is because there is no light in them" (Isa. 8:20). No matter what may be the credentials of a religious leader, if he does not teach the truth of God's Word, he is a false teacher. "Beloved, believe not every spirit, but try the spirits whether they are of God; because many false prophets are gone out into the world" (1 John 4:1).

4. Hatred (1 Peter 5:8). Satan hates God and God's people (Rev. 12:17) and loves only himself. He is a murderer (John 8:44) and a destroyer (Rev. 9:11; both "Abaddon" and "Apollyon" mean "destruction").

Hating evil is a holy hatred that is born of God: "Ye that love the Lord, hate evil" (Ps. 97:10). But most of the hatred in this world is displayed against good, not evil. People love the darkness and hate the light (see John 3:19–21). The world hated Christ when He was here, and it hates His followers (John 15:18). Hatred is usually born of fear and blindness. Satan uses his weapons of lies to blind men's minds, and his weapon of fear to control men's hearts, and the result is hatred. A famous poet has written, "Short is the road that leads from fear to hate."

Jonathan Swift, who wrote *Gulliver's Travels*, once said, "We have just enough religion to make us hate, but not enough to make us love one another." Jesus has but one way to destroy Satan's weapon of hatred, and that is love. He revealed His love for us when He died on the cross (Rom. 5:8). When someone trusts Christ as Saviour, He gives him His Holy Spirit within and "the love of God is shed abroad in our hearts" (Rom. 5:5). We are "taught of God to love one another" (1 Thes. 4:9). Not only are we to love one another, but we are also to love our enemies and those who hate us (Matt. 5:43–48).

Of all hatred, religious hatred is the worst. It is one of Satan's chief weapons to destroy God's work on earth. Professed Christians who hate one another usually disguise their hatred under a zeal for truth or purity. The Pharisees crucified Jesus because they felt He was leading the people astray. Their zeal for power and prestige made them the murderers of their own Messiah. Family fights, church splits, and many other personal squabbles are often subtly used by Satan to achieve his purposes, but to the human eye, such conflicts may seem like battles for the truth.

Three stages in Christ's war against Satan have been considered: He invaded Satan's territory, overcame Satan's power, and destroyed Satan's weapons. A fourth stage involves the spoils of this war.

Christ Claimed Satan's Spoils

"He . . . divideth his spoils" (v.22). This is what war is all about. It was Senator William L. Marcy who said, "To the victor belongs the spoils of the enemy!" He was referring to political victories in which the winners get to fill the offices with their friends, but the principle can be applied to other areas as well. Achan got into trouble because he *claimed* the spoils (Josh. 7:21ff), and Abraham stayed out of trouble because he *refused* the spoils (Gen. 14:21–24). But generally speaking, it is the privilege of the victor to claim and distribute the spoils. In fact, there are definite laws in the Old Testament governing the handling of the spoils of battle (Num. 31:25ff; 1 Sam. 30:24–25).

We should capture and use for God's glory everything Satan has possessed. The spoils referred to in this parable primarily mean *people who have been under Satan's control*. Jesus Christ came to "preach deliverance to the captives, and recovering of sight to the blind, to set at liberty them that are bruised" (Luke 4:18). Paul wrote that God "Hath delivered us from the power of darkness, and hath translated us into the kingdom of His dear Son" (Col. 1:13). This was one of the great consequences of Christ's work on the cross. Isaiah prophesied, "Therefore will I divide Him a portion with the great, and He shall divide the spoil with the strong" (Isa. 53:12).

Jesus invaded Satan's territory at His birth, and overcame his power and destroyed his weapons with His life, teaching, death, and resurrection. It was at His ascension that He took the spoils for Himself. The psalmist predicted, "Thou hast ascended on high, thou hast led captivity captive: Thou hast received gifts for men" (Ps. 68:18). Paul used this verse in Ephesians 4:8 and connected it with Christ's ascension.

In other words, having won the victory, Christ is now on the throne, claiming the spoils and distributing gifts. It is a picture of an eastern monarch sharing his spoils of war with those who helped him win the battle. But the difference is that Christ's spoils are the people who were at one time fighting against Him. He has set them free from Satan's dominion, and now they are enjoying their spiritual wealth in Christ.

The Apostle Paul is perhaps the best example of this truth. As Saul of Tarsus, he thought he was doing God a service when he persecuted the church and even voted to kill the saints. Like many stubborn religious people today who have never been born again, Saul's self-righteousness blinded him to his real need. When the Lord saved him and set him free, Saul of Tarsus, the dedicated rabbi, became Paul, the Apostle of the grace of God. Jesus then sent Paul into a world of lost sinners "to open their eyes, and to turn them from darkness to light, and from the power of Satan unto God" (Acts 26:18).

The big question is this: How shall you and I respond to this victory that Christ has won at the cost of His own blood? One thing is sure: *we cannot be neutral*. The parable of the empty house warns us against neutrality (Luke 11:23–26). Just as nature abhors a vacuum, so *spiritual* nature abhors a vacuum. No one can remain neutral, but must choose whom he will serve (see Josh. 24:15).

Either we are with Him, helping to gather the spoils, or we are against Him, helping Satan to scatter the spoils. There is no middle ground. If we are with Him, then we are on the winning side. If we are against Him, we are on the losing side. And one of these days, He shall return to earth to finish the war. Satan will be cast into hell (Rev. 20:10), sinners will be judged (Rev. 20:11–15), and Jesus Christ will usher in the new heaven and the new earth.

Have You Met Yourself in This Parable?

1. Did you realize that there is a spiritual war going on?

2. How have you responded to Christ's victories over Satan? Are you a part of this victory?

3. Are there areas in your life where you are attempting to be neutral?

4. Are you ever guilty of using Satan's weapons?

Luke 12:13–21

[13]And one of the company said unto Him, "Master, speak to my brother, that he divide the inheritance with me." [14]And He said unto him, "Man, who made me a judge or a divider over you?" [15]And He said unto them, "Take heed, and beware of covetousness: for a man's life consisteth not in the abundance of the things which he possesseth." [16]And He spake a parable unto them, saying, "The ground of a certain rich man brought forth plentifully: [17]And he thought within himself, saying, 'What shall I do, because I have no room where to bestow my fruits?' [18]And he said 'This will I do: I will pull down my barns, and build greater; and there will I bestow all my fruits and my goods. [19]And I will say to my soul, "Soul, thou hast much goods laid up for many years; take thine ease, eat, drink, and be merry." ' [20]But God said unto him, 'Thou fool, this night thy soul shall be required of thee: then whose shall these things be, which thou hast provided?' [21]So is he that layeth up treasure for himself, and is not rich toward God."

10
The Failure of Success
The Parable of the Foolish Farmer

Many of Christ's choicest teachings were given in response to some kind of interruption. In the situation described in Luke 12:13–21, He was teaching His disciples to fear God alone and trust Him for everything, when a man interrupted with a request for Jesus to settle a family quarrel. Apparently, he was a younger brother and his elder brother would not give him the one-third of the estate that was rightfully his.

You cannot help but feel sorry for this younger brother, *not* because he had not received his money, but because his spiritual condition was so degenerate. He was speaking when he should have been listening (check James 1:19). His desire for material things had choked the Word that Christ was sowing in his heart (Matt. 13:22). And he was applying the Word to others, not to himself.

Jesus could have settled the family dispute with great wisdom and skill, but He refused to do so. There are many people who want Jesus to solve their problems *but not to change their hearts*. Jesus knew that this family feud over money was only a symptom of a greater problem of *covetousness*. The Lord dealt with causes, not symptoms, and led Him to give this parable about the foolish farmer.

Covetousness is a desire for things and it can be the beginning of all kinds of sin. Eve coveted being like God and took the forbidden fruit. Lot's wife coveted Sodom and was killed on the spot. Achan coveted some spoils of war and destroyed himself and his family. David coveted his neighbor's wife and plunged himself, his family, and his nation into trouble. The last of the Ten Commandments is, "Thou shalt not covet." By coveting, we can break all the other nine Commandments.

The key to this parable is verse 15: "Take heed, and beware of covetousness: for a man's life consisteth not in the abundance of the things which he possesseth." The covetous person thinks that an *abundance of things* is the key to a successful life, but in this parable Jesus warned that an abundance of things could make a person a failure. The younger brother thought his troubles would be over if he received his inheritance. This does not mean God is insensitive to people's need for the essentials of life, for "your Father knoweth that ye have need of these things" (Luke 12:30). But it does mean that *of themselves* things cannot make life successful.

In the parable, Jesus pictured a man who suddenly became very wealthy. For the first time in his life he had an abundance of things. Unfortunately, he responded to these blessings the wrong way and died leaving everything behind for his family to fight over. This parable can be used as a spiritual inventory for examining our hearts. What responses do *we* make as we look at the material blessings of life?

Do We See God or Ourselves?
As this farmer beheld his bumper crop, he did not see the hand of God—he saw only himself. There are 11 personal pronouns in this man's speech to himself. He

had "I" trouble! "My goods . . . my fruits . . . my barns . . . my soul." He forgot that he was not the owner but only the possessor and the steward. All he had belonged to God.

The material blessings of life come from God. God made all things, and He made them good (Gen. 1:31). He knows that we need things (Luke 12:30), and He provides for us "all things richly to enjoy" (1 Tim. 6:17). God makes the sun to rise on the evil and the good, and He makes the rain to fall on the just and the unjust (Matt. 5:45). The fact that this farmer had such a rich harvest did not prove he was a better man. It simply proved that God was kind and gracious to him. Wealth is no measure of worth. Having a lot of money does not make a person worthy, nor does poverty mean a man is unworthy.

The person who looks at himself and forgets God when blessings are abundant is only revealing his pride. Peter had just the opposite experience when he caught that multitude of fish. He said, "Depart from me, for I am a sinful man, O Lord!" (Luke 5:8). Jacob had a similar experience, and prayed: "I am not worthy of the least of all the mercies, and of all the truth, which Thou has showed unto Thy servant" (Gen. 32:10). David responded to God's blessings by saying, "Who am I, O Lord God, and what is my house, that Thou hast brought me this far?" (2 Sam. 7:18, NASB)

The material blessings of life are either a *mirror* in which we see ourselves, or a *window* through which we see God. The proud selfish person thinks he deserves all these blessings and thinks only of himself. The person who knows that all blessings come from God looks away from himself to the Lord who gives so richly. For that matter, we ought to see the hand of God in a piece of bread as much as in a field of grain. Jesus saw His Father's goodness in the beautiful lily and the lowly sparrows.

No wonder Moses warned his people to prepare themselves for the blessings of the Promised Land. He knew they could face the battles and the burdens, but he was not sure they knew how to handle the blessings. "And it shall be, when the Lord thy God shall have brought thee into the land which He sware unto thy fathers . . . to give thee great and goodly cities, which thou buildest not, and houses full of all good things, which thou filledst not, vineyards and olive trees, which thou plantedst not; when thou shalt have eaten and be full; then beware lest thou forget the Lord, which brought thee forth out of the land of Egypt, from the house of bondage" (Deut. 6:10–12).

When we look at the blessings of life, do we instinctively think of God, or of ourselves? Is it an opportunity to inflate our egos, or do we feel greatly humbled that God should choose us to receive these blessings? This is what it means to be "rich toward God" (Luke 12:21). It means the material blessings of life enrich us spiritually instead of robbing us. We enjoy the material blessings *more* because they draw us closer to the Lord.

Do We Think of Enjoyment or Investment?
The self-centered person immediately thinks of enjoyment when he is blessed with material things: "take thine ease, eat, drink, and be merry" (v. 19). The spiritually-minded person would think of investment, asking, "How can I use these gifts to help others and glorify God?"

There is certainly nothing wrong with enjoyment. As we have noted, God gives to us "all things richly to enjoy" (1 Tim. 6:17). But *selfish* enjoyment that ignores God and others is not in the will of God. One of the tests of spiritual maturity is a desire to use what we have for others. The father who receives a surprise bonus at work and immediately thinks of what he can do for his family is giving evidence of love and maturity.

Jesus made it clear that an abundance of things is no guarantee of true life. Things are necessary to sustain physical life but they cannot satisfy the deeper spiritual life within. A vast difference exists between making a living and making a life.

Things cannot of themselves give *depth* to our lives. In fact, the people who live for things are usually very shallow. They live by what they see and measure everything in terms of their own enjoyment. *Length* of life is not guaranteed by things. While the wealthy man can purchase excellent medical care, this is no proof that he will live any longer than the poor man. The farmer in the parable had everything all planned—and that night he died.

Things cannot promise you any *breadth* of life. Imagine being able to put your life into barns! The Bible teaches, and it has been the experience of godly people through the ages, that a lust for things makes a person smaller in those areas of life that really count. A man's *height* is not changed by his possession of things. Jesus emphasized this when He asked, "And which of you with taking thought can add to his stature one cubit?" (Luke 12:25)

True stature and depth of life come from within. Godly character is not the result of the accumulation of things but the result of sacrifices and decisions in the will of God. Abraham was a wealthy man but he still walked with God and lived a life of faith. Lot coveted the things of the world and lost his wife, his home, and his position.

As we learned from the parable of the unjust

steward, we can take three approaches to life. Like the prodigal son, we can *waste* life. Like his elder brother, we can merely *spend* our lives. Or, like the steward, we can learn to *invest* our lives. The same Scripture that encourages us to enjoy the things God gives us also admonishes us to *employ* these things for the good of others and the glory of God: "That they do good, that they be rich in good works, ready to distribute, willing to communicate [share]; laying up in store for themselves a good foundation against the time to come, that they may lay hold on eternal life" (1 Tim. 6:18–19).

Consider what this farmer might have done, had he been a man of faith and dedication. He might have called his family and friends together and led them in a praise service, glorifying God for the rich harvest. He might have shared his wealth with those who were less fortunate. He might have distributed it to the members of his family to use while he was alive and not argue over it after he was dead. He might have invested that wealth in a wise way and used the income for worthy projects to make his community a better place to live.

We must think of life in terms of investment. This is what Jesus had in mind when He said, "Sell that ye have, and give alms; provide yourselves bags which wax not old, a treasure in the heavens that faileth not, where no thief approacheth, neither moth corrupt-eth" (Luke 12:33). Obviously, He is not telling us to go out of business and get rid of everything. He is urging us to invest in things eternal, and to use our wealth for that which cannot be stolen or destroyed. Jim Elliot, a missionary killed by the Indians he had gone to minister to, said it perfectly: "He is no fool to give what he cannot keep to gain what he cannot lose."

Do We Experience Anxiety or Peace?

People have the strange notion that things can give peace, when in reality things can create worry. Some of us can remember our excitement and feeling of security when we bought our first automobile. But we soon discovered that the many privileges of owning a car brought with them the headaches of taking care of it.

I do not agree with Henry Thoreau's pantheistic theology, but I do agree with some of his views of life. "A man is rich," he said, "in proportion to the number of things which he can afford to let alone." He wrote in his journal on March 11, 1856: "That man is the richest whose pleasures are cheapest."

King Solomon was a very wealthy man, yet his riches did not give him peace. "The sleep of a laboring man is sweet, whether he eat little or much: but the abundance of the rich will not suffer him to sleep" (Ecc. 5:12).

You will notice that Christ followed this parable with a sermon on *worry*. The poor think that the rich never worry, yet the rich have worries that the poor never dream of. Whether rich or poor, if we find ourselves worrying, it is a sign that we have the wrong attitude toward things. "What shall I do?" is the anxious cry of the person who lives for things.

Consider what Jesus taught about worry (vv. 22–34).

Worry is unreasonable (12:23). Life is more than food and clothing. To worry about things is to neglect what is most important—life itself. What good is an expensive wardrobe if the person wearing it is cheap and infantile? What good is a sumptuous feast if the persons eating it are starved morally and spiritually? It is unreasonable to worry about externals that cannot contribute to eternal things.

Worry is unnatural (12:24, 27). The ravens and the lilies do not worry. Why? Because all of nature knows that the Father will meet their needs. "He giveth to the beast his food, and to the young ravens which cry" (Ps. 147:9). And, "Thou openest Thine hand, and satisfiest the desire of every living thing." (Ps. 145:16). Even if a sparrow falls to the ground dead, it does not fall alone for the Father never forgets even a sparrow (Luke 12:6; Matt. 10:29).

Worry is unavailing (12:25-26). Worry cannot make us taller or help us live longer. In fact, it does just the opposite—it shortens our lives! Since worry does not accomplish anything good, why worry?

Worry is unnecessary (12:28). The fact that the Father takes care of us does not mean we should be careless or complacent, or that we should expect the Father to do for us what we must do for ourselves. But it does mean that He cares for us because we are valuable to Him. He cares for the grass, the flowers, and the birds, and surely He will care for His children.

Worry is unspiritual (12:29-30). The unbelievers of the world have a right to worry, but Christians are different from them. Christians have a heavenly Father who cares for them, so any worrying is an evidence of unbelief and a poor witness to the world.

What is the cure for worry? Stop living for things and start living for God. "But rather seek ye the kingdom of God; and all these things shall be added unto you" (Luke 12:31). Nothing simplifies life like putting God first and getting your priorities straight. If the abundance or lack of things robs us of peace, then we are not wholly yielded to God. This may be a symptom of covetousness. On the other hand, we must avoid the *false peace* that can come with prosperity. "I have it made!" said the farmer. "I can take it easy!" If your peace is based on things, and not on the will of God, you have a false peace.

Three questions have been asked in our personal inventory: When we look at the material blessings of life, do we see God or ourselves? Do we think of enjoyment or investment? Do we experience anxiety or peace? There is a fourth question.

Do We Think of Security or Insecurity?

A worldly-minded person looks at material things and immediately thinks of security. Now he can take it easy and not work so hard; now he can pay his bills and enjoy life. But there is no security in things. In fact, things are deceptive: they appear to be satisfying and lasting when they are actually temporary and unable to satisfy the deepest needs of life.

The farmer was basking in *false success*. In the eyes of man he was wise and successful but in the eyes of God he was a fool and a failure. He had the things that money could buy, but he lost the things that money cannot buy. True success is not measured in wealth alone. Jesus and His apostles were poor, and yet who would doubt their success in the eyes of God? It is too bad that so many people measure success by prices instead of values.

The farmer was enjoying a *false satisfaction*. Imagine trying to satisfy your soul with goods from a barn! Wise King Solomon discovered that entertainment, accomplishment, and the enrichment of wealth could not satisfy the deep cravings of the human heart (Ecc. 2:1–11). His conclusion was "Behold, all was vanity and vexation of spirit!" False satisfaction only encourages false success, and both encourage *false security*.

"Soul, thou has much goods laid up for many years!" (Luke 12:19) Many years! *That very night he died.* No doubt, after the funeral, some curious businessman asked, "And how much did he leave behind?" The answer: *everything*. He could have sent it ahead had he lived for God.

Jesus Christ saw no security in things. He knew that material things could rust, that moths and other creatures could destroy, and that thieves could steal. He knew that men could die and never again have the use of that wealth. Was He being unduly pessimistic and gloomy when He said these things? Of course not. He was simply being realistic and trying to keep us from building our lives on the sand. Jesus wants us to remember that the only true security is in the will of God.

It is not sinful to provide for the future. Paul wrote, "For the children ought not to lay up for the parents, but the parents for the children" (2 Cor. 12:14). Israel would have been destroyed as a nation had not Joseph stored up food. The Christian can live only a day at a time, but he must remind himself that he cannot boast of tomorrow even though he has planned and prepared for tomorrow. (Read Proverbs 27:1 and James 4:13–15.) "If the Lord wills" must always be the attitude of a believer.

Certainly, God wants us to enjoy the blessings of life. There is nothing spiritual about sitting morosely in a corner and saying, "These things will not last anyway! Why enjoy them?" God wants us to enjoy His good gifts, just as we want our children to enjoy what we give them. But He does not want us to *depend* on things—He wants us to depend on Him.

The answer to worry and insecurity is: "Fear not, little flock; for it is your Father's good pleasure to give you the kingdom" (Luke 12:32). Dr. G. Campbell Morgan pointed out that Jesus was not mixing His metaphors in this statement, for middle eastern sheiks would be shepherds, fathers, and kings at the same time. As believers in Jesus Christ, we are sheep in God's flock, children in God's family, and citizens in God's kingdom. We have nothing to fear.

It is all a matter of the heart. Jesus said, "For where your treasure is, there will your heart be also" (Matt. 6:21). The eyes see what the heart loves. If we love God and put His will first in our lives, then whatever material blessings we receive will only draw us closer to Him. Wealth will be our servant, not our master, and we will invest in things eternal.

Have You Met Yourself in This Parable?

1. How did you respond to this man's windfall? Did you say, "What a fortunate fellow!" or "You had better watch out"?

2. What was your response to his decision to build and save?

3. Do you agree with his philosophy of life? Defend your position.

4. How did you respond to the man's sudden death? What do you think was the greatest tragedy in his death?

5. Can people tell in your life whether or not money is your servant or your master?

6. How do you measure success?

Matthew 18:21–35

²¹Then came Peter to Him, and said, "Lord, how oft shall my brother sin against me, and I forgive him? till seven times?" ²²Jesus saith unto him, "I say not unto thee, until seven times: but, until seventy times seven. ²³Therefore is the kingdom of heaven likened unto a certain king, which would take account of his servants. ²⁴And when he had begun to reckon, one was brought unto him, which owed him ten thousand talents. ²⁵But forasmuch as he had not to pay, his lord commanded him to be sold, and his wife, and children, and all that he had, and payment to be made. ²⁶The servant therefore fell down, and worshiped him, saying 'Lord, have patience with me, and I will pay thee all.' ²⁷Then the lord of that servant was moved with compassion, and loosed him, and forgave him the debt. ²⁸But the same servant went out, and found one of his fellowservants, which owed him an hundred pence: and he laid hands on him, and took him by the throat, saying 'Pay me that thou owest.' ²⁹And his fellowservant fell down at his feet, and besought him, saying 'Have patience with me, and I will pay thee all.' ³⁰But he would not: but went and cast him into prison, till he should pay the debt. ³¹So when his fellowservants saw what was done, they were very sorry, and came and told unto their lord all that was done. ³²Then his lord, after that he had called him, said unto him, 'O thou wicked servant, I forgave thee all that debt, because thou desiredst me: ³³shouldest not thou also have had compassion on thy fellowservant, even as I had pity on thee?' ³⁴And his lord was wroth, and delivered him to the tormentors, till he should pay all that was due unto him. ³⁵So likewise shall My heavenly Father do also unto you, if ye from your hearts forgive not every one his brother their trespasses"

11

The World's Worst Prison
The Parable of the Unmerciful Servant

The official Spanish name for the site is the Isle of the Pelicans, but nobody knows it by that name. It is best known as Alcatraz, one of the most escape-proof prisons in the world. From 1933 to 1963 it served as a federal prison, and during that time 26 prisoners tried to escape but only five succeeded. Surrounded by the cold waters of San Francisco Bay, Alcatraz boasted high walls, double-lock doors, machine guns in the hands of the guards, and a staff that could not be bribed. Alcatraz is now a tourist attraction, but some tourists have admitted they do not find the Big House too attractive.

The world's worst prison, however, is not Alcatraz or Devil's Island, for those places can only confine the body. The prison Jesus talked about in this parable shackles the *inner man* and sad to say, *we put ourselves into this prison*. What is this terrible prison? It is created by the person who will not forgive his brother. It is the dungeon of an unforgiving spirit.

The best way to understand the parable of the unmerciful servant is to consider it from three different viewpoints: its setting, its meaning, and (most important) living out its teaching.

The Setting of the Parable

The disciples' question, "Who is the greatest in the kingdom of heaven?" grew out of an argument that seems to have been an important one to the disciples, for you find it recurring in the Gospel records.

Instead of naming one of the disciples, Jesus pointed to a little child and named him as the greatest in the kingdom. It was a telling lesson in humility, and a lesson we still need today. A child exhibits beautiful humility in the way he accepts himself and others, trusts others, and appreciates others.

But humility was only the first lesson—the second followed immediately. The Lord taught them to be open and honest with each other and confess their sins and seek forgiveness (Matt. 18:15–20). If this instruction were followed in our local churches, we would see most of the personal problems solved. The first step in solving a personal difference is to go to the person who has offended you. Keep the matter private. If that does not work, go back again and take one or two believers along to pray and counsel. If that fails, then the issue must be taken to the church. Note the tragedy of unforgiven sin: first two people are involved, then three or four, then the whole congregation! When sin is not dealt with, it spreads.

At this point, Peter had a problem, so he shared it with the Lord. "How often shall my brother sin against me, and I forgive him? Till seven times?" (This was being generous. The rabbis advised forgiving a brother only three times. They based it on Job 33:29–30, which reads in the Hebrew: "Lo, God does all these things twice, three times with man, to bring back his soul from the pit.")

It is important to note the mistakes that Peter revealed in his question. He assumed that his brother would sin against him, not he against his brother.

Peter had missed the lesson on humility. Then, Peter wanted some kind of rule to guide him in his personal relationships with other believers. He wanted to be able to *measure* forgiveness. This meant he was thinking of setting a limit: "This far and no farther!" The Lord exposed that fallacy when He said, "Not seven times, but seventy times seven!" By the time you have forgiven somebody that many times, you are in the habit of forgiving and will not need to obey rules or set limits.

Of course, Jesus was not recommending a shallow, indiscriminate kind of forgiveness that really is no forgiveness at all. True forgiveness is based on what He taught in verses 15–20. There cannot be true forgiveness unless sin is confessed and dealt with. In these verses, Jesus describes a local fellowship where there is love, unity, prayer, and an atmosphere of brotherly kindness. Forgiveness is not cheap. It cost God His Son that He might be able to forgive us.

Jesus told this parable against a background of argument, humility, and forgiveness. To understand the parable, we need to remember three things.

1. Christ was talking about forgiveness, not salvation. The king in the story is not a picture of God, for God does not forgive one day and condemn the next. Salvation is a once-for-all experience that does not change, even though the enjoyment of it may change from day to day.

2. He was talking about brothers, not outsiders. Peter asked about forgiving *his brother* and Jesus reemphasized forgiving a brother (v. 35). This parable does not discuss God's forgiveness of the lost sinner, but the importance of brother forgiving brother in the family of God. Salvation is eternal, not temporary. We do not need to suffer torture to gain God's forgiveness.

3. This judgment is here and now, not in the future. Every problem that we face with another person is an opportunity for growth or judgment. If we obey God, we will grow. If we disobey, we will be judged. In fact, *we judge ourselves.* The man in the parable *put himself* into prison. We must not project this experience into the future. Here and now, we are either forgiving or unforgiving, and we experience the consequences.

The Meaning of the Parable

It was not unusual for kings to audit their books to see if their stewards had been faithful. Imagine the king's surprise when he discovered that one of his subjects had been repeatedly borrowing from him and owed him 10,000 talents. To understand the buying power of a talent, consider the fact that one talent would purchase a slave. The total annual tax bill for Palestine was about 800 talents, and this man owed 10,000 talents! One talent would be equivalent to 20 years' wages for the average man.

The king forgave his servant because he had compassion on him and his family. The servant begged to be given time to repay, but he did not explain how he would secure such a large amount of money. His release was solely on the basis of his lord's compassionate heart. You would expect the forgiven servant to go out and joyfully share this experience with others, but he did not. Instead, he arrested a man who owed him a small amount (about four months' wages) and threw him into prison. There was obviously something wrong with the forgiven servant's heart, and this is the major emphasis of the story. Christ taught that there are three levels of forgiveness.

1. Receiving forgiveness. "I forgive you all that

debt!" the king said to his servant, and the servant got up from the floor and walked out a free man. He had received forgiveness. This forgiveness was not cheap, for his lord lost a great amount of money which would never be paid back. The servant did not earn the pardon—he deserved to be punished for what he had done. The forgiveness the man received was the result of his lord's compassionate heart.

If a despotic earthly lord can do this, how much more does our Father in heaven forgive us when we come to Him? How much people owe God for His patience, mercy, and longsuffering! God sends His rain and sunshine on all kinds of undeserving people, yet they take it for granted. Furthermore, God has given certain laws that He wants obeyed, and every act of disobedience makes a person that much more obligated to God. People are in debt to God and He expects them to pay.

But sinners are bankrupt. They may, like the man in the story, defend themselves and promise to pay their debts, but they cannot. If people are forgiven at all, it is because God assumes the loss, pays the debt, and graciously grants His salvation. And the forgiveness that God grants is not temporary or conditional—it is free and eternal. If you have trusted Jesus Christ, you have received forgiveness. "To Him [Jesus] give all the prophets witness, that through His name whosoever believeth in Him shall receive remission of sins" (Acts 10:43). "And their sins and their iniquities will I remember no more" (Heb. 10:17).

2. *Experiencing forgiveness.* Receiving a gift is one thing, but it is quite another matter to have the gift do something in your heart. Forgiveness can be a routine event instead of a true heart experience. It takes more than receiving a gift to change a life. In

fact, if the heart is not in it, receiving the gift could actually make a person worse instead of better. This is what happened to the servant in the parable. Instead of making him more loving and forgiving, the experience hardened him and injured others.

The fact that we have been forgiven ought to make us better persons in every way. Forgiveness must not be only a past event in history, but a present experience in daily reality. *A person who has been set free ought not to live as though he were still in prison.* Certainly, there ought to be in our hearts a deep love for God who has forgiven us, and for His children as well. (It should not be difficult for the forgiven to love the forgiven!) It is not enough only to *receive* forgiveness—we must also *experience* forgiveness in our hearts.

The Lord uses various means to help us experience forgiveness. Whenever the church family meets for Communion, the bread and the cup remind us of the price He paid for our forgiveness. When we remember Him we remember what He did for us. As we read the Bible daily and meditate on its truths, we should let the Holy Spirit make these truths real in our hearts. We must never get to the place in life where we take forgiveness for granted.

But one of the most effective ways God has for keeping us forgiveness-conscious is our relationships with other believers. When others sin against us we must forgive them, remembering that we have been forgiven ourselves. In the daily pressures and disagreements of life, we have many reminders of what God has done for us.

3. *Sharing forgiveness.* Not only do we *receive* forgiveness and *experience* it in our hearts, but we must *share* it with others. The forgiven servant would not forgive his fellowservant! Peter was willing to

forgive a man seven times, but the servant would not even forgive one time! As a consequence, the servant was thrown back into prison, along with his family, and all of them had to suffer.

We are the losers if we do not forgive others. We may think that we are hurting *them*, but in reality we are only hurting *ourselves* and our loved ones. Paul wrote, "Be ye kind one to another, tenderhearted, forgiving one another, even as God for Christ's sake hath forgiven you" (Eph. 4:32). And, "Forbearing one another, and forgiving one another, if any man have a quarrel against any: even as Christ forgave you, so also do ye" (Col. 3:13).

We have nothing to lose and everything to gain when we practice forgiveness. The servant in the parable did not share forgiveness—he shared anger and violence and condemnation. What was wrong with him? He had not truly experienced forgiveness in his heart so he had nothing to share. Judicially, he was a forgiven man but practically, he was still a criminal and a prisoner. A careful reading of verse 26 reveals that this servant lacked everything necessary for a deep experience of forgiveness.

To begin with, he was not really convinced that he was a sinner. He had been caught, and he was sorry that he had been caught, *but he was not sorry that he had sinned*. He was willing for his lord to forgive him, but he was not willing to admit that he had done wrong. There can be no deep experience of forgiveness until first there is a deep sense of sin and need.

When our children were small, they would sometimes hurt one another, as all children will do. My wife and I would try to explain the wrong done, and then we would say to the offender, "Now, you apologize to your brother (or sister)," and the response would be a very sullen and bitter, "I'm sorry."

Children do not usually grasp the meaning of either sin or forgiveness, and their confessions are not very deep.

But there was something else wrong with this man. He was proud and thought he could handle the debt himself. How long did he think he would have to work to be able to pay back that much money? He was bluffing, of course, trying to talk his way out of the situation, and he went away thinking he had succeeded. "What a clever fellow I am!" he said to himself, and perhaps to his family. "I convinced that man to cancel the debt!" No sense of remorse or repentance was evident. He did not grasp the price the lord had to pay or the depth of compassion the lord revealed. The entire experience was self-centered. The servant left the throne-room with an inflated ego, not a humble spirit.

Note one more fact about this servant: he lived in the realm of *justice*, not *mercy*. He was glad to have mercy for himself and his family, but he did not want mercy for any of his debtors. When he met the man who owed him a small amount, the servant immediately became policeman, judge, and jury. His motive was revenge, and revenge cannot live in the same heart as forgiveness. He had just been forgiven a debt of $2,000,000 (in modern terms to show the proportions), but he could not forgive his fellow–servant a debt of $20.

The lesson is clear: you cannot share forgiveness unless you have received it *and* experienced it. Forgiveness must go deeper than the hands or the lips—it must possess and transform the heart. If we do not forgive, we put ourselves into prison, and we take others there with us. In my pastoral ministry, I have met families who lived in an emotional and spiritual prison because of parents who were unforgiving, judgmental, and condemning. God will not prevent us from going to prison (see verse 35). He cannot answer our prayers when we have an unforgiving spirit. (See Mark 11:25 and Psalm 66:18.)

Living the Parable

Perhaps the best way to apply this parable to our lives is to take inventory of our hearts.

1. *Have you received forgiveness?* You do this by trusting Jesus Christ as your Saviour. Forgiveness is not earned, but is a gift from God to those who receive His Son. Forgiveness is not deserved, so do not come to God and tell Him how good you are.

2. *Have you experienced forgiveness?* Has your heart been broken as you have contemplated God's great love and mercy toward you? Have you calculated your spiritual debt to God? One of the evidences of experiencing forgiveness is the constant wonder in your heart, "Why should He save *me?*" Another evidence is a tenderness toward others, in spite of their sins. When you find yourself getting a hard heart and a judicial spirit, you need to get alone with the Lord and experience again the depth of His forgiveness. Remember that every abrasive experience with other people is an opportunity to experience forgiveness in a deeper way.

3. *Are you sharing forgiveness?* All day long we need to forgive people in our hearts. We may not be able to forgive them to their faces (such as the driver who almost sideswipes your car or the person who makes that abusive phone call and hangs up), but we must forgive them from our hearts. To harbor a hateful spirit will put you into prison.

The test of forgiveness is freedom. The person who harbors resentment and carries grudges is never free. He is living in a prison of his own feelings and frustrations. Forgiveness always brings out the best in us, but an attitude of condemnation and revenge always brings out the worst in us. Forgiveness means we are living by grace, but revenge means we are living under the Law. If we try to put other people under the Law by refusing to forgive them, we should not be surprised to find ourselves in prison too.

An unforgiving heart always experiences torment. The lord delivered the servant to the tormentors. This word carries the idea of inner mental torment as much as physical torture. I have met Christians who carry grudges, and in counseling them, I have discovered how miserable they really are. Instead of loving and using their energy for creative ministry, they are hating and wasting their energy on enemies they cannot fight. It is a useless cause. How much better they would be if they would forgive those who have wronged them. They—and their families— would experience a joy and freedom that comes only when they forgive as God has forgiven them.

We ought to forgive from our hearts and, if possible, go to the person and seek personal forgiveness. Even if the person does not forgive us, or accept our forgiveness, we will experience God's blessing in our lives.

I think that the cathedral in Coventry, England is the most beautiful I have ever seen in that land of monuments. The design and colors are breathtaking. But the beauty of the cathedral is augmented by the presence next door of the ruins of the old cathedral, bombed during World War II. As we walked across the stone floor of that ruined building, we noticed the inscription behind the altar: "Father, forgive them." We were told by the guide that many German Christians assisted in the building of the new cathedral. It is a monument to Christian forgiveness and brotherhood.

Have You Met Yourself in This Parable?
Is there anybody you need to forgive?

²⁷Then answered Peter and said unto Him, "Behold, we have forsaken all, and followed Thee; what shall we have therefore?" ²⁸And Jesus said unto them, "Verily I say unto you, that ye which have followed Me, in the regeneration when the Son of man shall sit in the throne of His glory, ye also shall sit upon twelve thrones, judging the twelve tribes of Israel. ²⁹And every one that hath forsaken houses, or brethren, or sisters, or father, or mother, or wife, or children, or lands, for My name's sake, shall receive an hundredfold, and shall inherit everlasting life. ³⁰But many that are first shall be last; and the last shall be first. ²⁰⁺¹For the kingdom of heaven is like unto a man that is a householder, which went out early in the morning to hire laborers into his vineyard. ²And when he had agreed with the laborers for a penny a day, he sent them into his vineyard. ³And he went out about the third hour, and saw others standing idle in the marketplace, ⁴and said unto them; 'Go ye also into the vineyard, and whatsoever is right I will give you.' And they went their way. ⁵Again he went out about the sixth and ninth hour, and did likewise. ⁶And about the eleventh hour he went out, and found others standing idle, and saith unto them, 'Why stand ye here all the day idle?' ⁷They say unto him, 'Because no man hath hired us.' He saith unto them, 'Go ye also into the vineyard; and whatsoever is right, that shall ye receive.' ⁸So when even was come, the lord of the vineyard saith unto his steward, 'Call the laborers, and give them their hire, beginning from the last unto the first.' ⁹And when they came that were hired about the eleventh hour, they received every man a penny. ¹⁰But when the first came, they supposed that they should have received more; and they likewise received every man a penny. ¹¹And when they had received it, they murmured against the goodman of the house, ¹²saying, 'These last have wrought but one hour, and thou has made them equal unto us, which have borne the burden and heat of the day.' ¹³But he answered one of them and said, 'Friend, I do thee no wrong: didst not thou agree with me for a penny? ¹⁴Take that thine is, and go thy way: I will give unto this last, even as unto thee. ¹⁵Is it not lawful for me to do what I will with mine own? Is thine eye evil, because I am good?' ¹⁶So the last shall be first, and the first last: for many be called, but few chosen."

12

How Much Will We Get?
The Parable of the Laborers in the Vineyard

President William McKinley once wrote to Senator Henry Cabot Lodge, "For Labor, a short day is better than a short dollar." What would he say to the men in this story who had a *long* day and a short dollar? In fact, many features in this parable seem to contradict what you and I know about modern labor and management in today's society. Apparently, there are no seniority rights in this vineyard, and a person's wages are fixed no matter how long he works. Some workers received a day's wages for an hour's labor!

We must not jump to the conclusion that Jesus did not know what He was talking about, or that He stretched the truth in order to make a point. He was a keen observer of the ways of men. He had often seen the laborers in the marketplace, waiting for someone to hire them. He had heard the haggling over wages and the complaining at the end of the hard day. Jesus labored as a carpenter for many years, and His daily experience was with the laboring man.

It is important to note that this parable is not talking about *salvation*. To make the penny (a day's wage) stand for salvation is to miss the whole meaning of the story. Nobody works for salvation, and certainly nobody is going to complain about his own salvation or someone else's. To use the different hours of the day to symbolize ages at which people respond to Christ's call is wrong. We sometimes say, "She was saved at the eleventh hour," meaning that the person turned to Christ just before it was too late. But the parable is not telling us how to get saved.

Nor is Christ dealing with gaining *rewards*. Rewards are granted to His own on the basis of faithfulness and service, and each man's reward is different. "And every man shall receive his own reward according to his own labor" (1 Cor. 3:8). That certainly did not happen in this parable! Some men toiled under the hot sun for 12 hours and received a denarius (a penny—a coin that looked like the American dime), while others toiled for but one hour and received the same amount.

If Jesus was not talking about either salvation or rewards, what was He talking about? He was warning His disciples about a wrong attitude in service. The setting of the parable (Matt. 19:16–30) makes this clear. The rich young man who came to Jesus refused to give his all and follow Christ, so he went away in great disappointment. At that point, Jesus warned His disciples against riches and the sad effects they can have on one's spiritual life.

Peter responded to Jesus' warning in a natural way. The rich young man had not forsaken all to follow Christ, but Peter and the other disciples *had* forsaken all. "What shall we have therefore?" Peter asked, and it was a logical question. The Lord's answer was encouraging: God would repay them a hundredfold for their sacrifice (imagine getting 100 percent return on your investment), and they would share thrones in the future kingdom.

But Jesus detected in Peter's question an attitude of heart that was dangerous. Was Peter serving the

Lord *only* for what he could get out of it? Were the disciples forsaking all *only* because He had promised them a reward? To counteract this subtle attitude of "What am I going to get?" the Lord told this parable; and in it, He gave several warnings that relate to Christian service.

Beware of Making Bargains with God

There were no labor organizations in that day. The day-laborers used to gather in the town marketplace early in the morning, and there the employers would hire them. Both day-laborers and soldiers were paid a denarius a day, and each man was paid at the close of the day. It was considered a great sin to hold back a man's wages, since most of them lived from day to day on their earnings and had no savings to tide them over. (See Deut. 24:15; James 5:1–4.)

The owner of the vineyard was anxious to get in his harvest before the rains. He went to the town labor pool at six o'clock in the morning and personally recruited some workers. But the harvest was great and the laborers few, so he had to return for more workers at nine o'clock, noon, and three o'clock in the afternoon. As the day drew to a close, he still needed a few more workers, so at five o'clock he hired the last group. We ought to commend the men in the last group for sticking it out and not getting discouraged when nobody hired them all day.

Did you notice that there were actually two kinds of workers? The men who were hired early in the morning would not go to work until they knew how much they would make. The owner agreed to pay them a denarius a day (vv. 2 and 13). But *the other workers had no contract*. They trusted the owner to give them what was right. "Go ye also into the vineyard, and whatsoever is right, I will give you"

(Matt. 20:4). They trusted the owner's word and character.

This explains why the owner paid the men in reverse order, starting with the last workers that were hired. He wanted the six o'clock workers to see how generous he was to employees who did not have a contract. When the early workers saw the five o'clock laborers receive a denarius, they joyfully assumed that they would receive 12 denarii, because they had worked 12 hours. The three o'clock crowd was paid a denarius each—this cut the wages down to four denarii for the early–morning workers. As each group was paid, these men saw their expected wages decrease until it was their turn in line, and each man received a denarius.

Of course, the men complained. Apparently, they sent one of their number to argue with the master, or perhaps the one the master addressed in verse 13 was the most vocal of the lot. But the men really had nothing to complain about because they received *exactly the amount they had bargained for* early that morning.

We can see how this applied to Peter. He wanted to know what he was going to get. He was signing a contract with the Lord. "Beware, Peter," Jesus was saying, "because you will get just what you bargain for. Why not trust Me to give you what is right?" We need this warning today: don't make bargains with God. Let God write the contract and pay the wages, for He is just and generous. If *we* write the contract and tell God what we want, *we will always be the losers*. But if we let Him do it His way, we will receive "exceedingly abundantly above all that [we] ask or think" (Eph. 3:20).

This means that we must trust the Lord and rely on His Word and character, for "Shall not the Judge of all the earth do right?" (Gen. 18:25). Our Master in heaven does not limit Himself to what is just and equal (Col. 4:1); He gives what is gracious and generous. The key phrase in Romans 5 is "much more" (vv. 9–10, 15, 17, 20). Jesus asked, "If ye then, being evil, know how to give good gifts unto your children, how much more shall your Father which is in heaven give good things to them that ask Him?" (Matt. 7:11). God will always give us "much more," so let Him write the contract.

Never be afraid of the will of God. He calls us personally (the owner did not send his foreman to hire the men), and He will see to it that we get a generous reward if we are faithful. God is more interested in our *heart attitudes* than in our work. If our hearts are right, our work will be right, but if our hearts are selfish and grasping, our work will suffer. Our relationships to the Master are most important. Do we trust Him? Do we believe His Word? Are we willing to work without a contract?

Beware of Watching Other Workers

Peter had watched the rich young ruler walk away from Jesus, and Peter contrasted himself with that unhappy man. The ruler was rich but Peter was poor. Although Peter had been a partner in a successful fishing business, he had given it all up to follow Jesus. But the rich man had given up nothing. Yet the rich man was still rich and Peter was still poor! Surely there would be some kind of compensation for the sacrifices Peter had made to follow Jesus.

The disciples were often guilty of watching other people and drawing wrong conclusions. They saw a man cast out demons in Jesus' name, but since the man did not belong to their group, they rebuked him. Jesus, however, rebuked them, "Forbid him not: for he that is not against us is for us" (Luke 9:50). The disciples had been unable to cast out a demon themselves (Luke 9:37–41), and yet they dared to criticize a believer who was able to do it. We too often attack those whose success exposes our own failures.

My family and I once lived on a street where one of the neighbors was a people-watcher. She would sit in the front room of her house with a pair of binoculars and survey the neighborhood. If we did not close the blinds on our front window, she would look right into our house. Sad to say, many Christians are people–watchers. Instead of keeping their eyes on the Master and seeking to please Him, they are spying on other saints and finding fault with them. Peter made this same mistake after he had been restored to fellowship following Christ's resurrection (John 21). Jesus said to Peter, "'Follow Me.' Then Peter, turning about, seeth the disciple whom Jesus loved following . . . Peter seeing him saith to Jesus, 'Lord, and what shall this man do?' Jesus saith unto him, 'If I will that he tarry till I come, what is that to thee? Follow thou Me'" (John 21:19–21).

When we get our eyes off the Lord and start watching other believers, certain definite symptoms show up in our lives. To begin with, we start to envy them and what they have. We start to get an "evil eye" (v. 15) so that we cannot see anything good about our fellow workers. Envy is a sin (Gal. 5:21), and it can lead to further sins. When we start comparing, we start coveting, and then we start *complaining*. The Christian who is a people-watcher is never satisfied with what God gives him but always wants what somebody else has.

All of this leads to a bitter attitude toward God. We get the feeling that God has given us a raw deal. We become like the elder brother in the parable of the prodigal son (Luke 15:11–32), "Lo, these many years do I serve thee." When our hearts become bitter against God, we are in danger of losing the blessings God has given us and the ones He wants to give us.

We must face the fact honestly that it is a sin for Christians to watch one another and judge one another. Certainly we need to *watch over* one another in tender love and seek to help one another. But that is a far cry from what the critical workers did in the parable. The other workers belong to God and not to us, and it is His job to evaluate their work and assign their wages. Paul asked, "Who art thou that judgest another man's servant? To his own master he standeth or falleth" (Rom. 14:4). And, "But why dost thou judge thy brother? Or why dost thou set at nought thy brother? For we shall all stand before the judgment seat of Christ" (Rom. 14:10).

Furthermore, when we keep our eyes on other Christians, they come between God and us. We are co-laborers with the Lord, not competitors against the Lord's people. The only way His servants can work effectively together is by all of them seeking to please the Master. But if our eyes are on the other workers and not on the Master, we are going to cause trouble and miss the blessings of effective service.

I recall an embarrassing experience I had while driving in Chicago. I noticed that a driver in the other lane was not driving safely. He would change lanes without signaling, for example, and on one occasion, he almost hit another car. I became so engrossed in this other driver that I almost caused an accident myself! I am not excusing either one of us, because we were both wrong, but I am blaming myself for not keeping my eyes where they belonged.

Another traffic experience comes to mind. At a certain busy intersection in Chicago, where three main streets meet, there is a double set of stop lights. The second set, perhaps 15 yards past the first set, controls the flow of traffic for the few cars who make it through the double intersection before the main light turns red. The first time I drove through that intersection, I almost jumped the gun because I was watching the wrong set of lights. Then I saw the sign: *Obey Your Own Signal.* Whenever I am tempted to watch other workers and get critical, I remember that sign. We must keep our eyes on Jesus Christ, seek only to please Him, and let Him do what He wills with and for other workers.

Beware of Overconfidence

"They supposed that they should have received more" (Matt. 20:10). These workers were overconfident and ended up being disappointed. We should always have confidence in God because He can be trusted. But we must never trust our own evaluations based on our short-sighted observations. These laborers negotiated their own contract but they did not want to stick to it.

But even Peter was overconfident. "Behold, we have forsaken all, and followed Thee; what shall we have therefore?" (Matt. 19:27) Jesus could have replied, "Peter, how do you know that you will have *anything*? Aren't you getting a bit overconfident?" Peter thought he was among the first, but Jesus warned that he might find himself among the last.

Whenever we are tempted to boast about our work, or belittle another's work, we ought to read 1 Corinthians 4:5, "Therefore judge nothing before the time, until the Lord come, who both will bring to light the hidden things of darkness, and will make manifest the counsels of the hearts: and then shall every man have praise of God." Whatever judgments we make today, either of ourselves or others, are bound to be faulty because we do not see men's hearts. We see the external actions but we cannot discern the hidden motives, *and it is the motive that determines the value of the ministry*. When Christ returns to judge our works there will be many surprises, for His judgment will be perfect and just.

At the beginning of the parable (Matt. 19:30), and at the end (Matt. 20:16), Jesus talked about the last being first and the first being last. What did He mean by this statement? It relates to the statement of the master in verse 8: "Give them their hire, beginning from the last unto the first." Jesus is warning us and encouraging us. Some who are first in their own eyes will be last in His eyes on that day, and some who are last in their own eyes will be first. Many faithful workers will discover their rewards are far greater than they ever could imagine. The praise of men, and the popularity of men, are no guarantee of God's approval.

We can be confident that God will give us far more than we deserve but we must not serve Him only for reward. The main lesson of this parable is that workers must watch their motives and be sure they are serving God because of their love for Him, and not because of a promised reward. It is possible to accomplish God's work and yet not really do God's will. The six o'clock workers got their work done, but they did not please their master. Instead, they criticized him for being so cheap. Like the prodigal's elder brother, they dutifully did their job, but their hearts were not in it.

Perhaps one of the best examples of this sinful attitude is the Prophet Jonah. When God called Jonah, he refused to work at all. God had to chasten him to bring him to the place of surrender. Jonah finally obeyed and went to Nineveh, but his heart was not in his ministry. He preached God's message faithfully, but all the while really longed for God's judgment to fall on Nineveh. He did God's work, but he was not in God's will, nor did he please God's heart. He obeyed because he was afraid not to obey. In the last chapter of the Book of Jonah, the truth came out that Jonah's heart was filled with bitter resentment and not God's love.

The workers who made a bargain with the master did not trust his word. When He said to the other workers, "Whatever is right, I will give you!" They believed him and joyfully entered into the work. They believed he was a generous and honest man and their faith was rewarded. They all received far more than they expected or deserved.

The last phrase in Matthew 20:16 is not found in some manuscripts, but since it is found in Matthew 22:14, we know it is part of inspired Scripture. D. L. Moody used to read this statement, "For many are called, but few are *choice*." He believed the word referred to the *quality* of people who really serve God in contrast to the many who are called and seem to be working for Him. I think his interpretation is a good one. There are ordinary servants of God, and there are choice servants of God.

Three warnings are given to heed as we serve the Lord: beware of making bargains with God, beware of watching other workers, and beware of getting over-confident. These warnings include three different relationships: with God, with our fellow-workers, and with ourselves. If we are right in our relationships with God then we will be right in our relationship to other workers and to ourselves. They go together.

The parable of the laborers in the vineyard grew out of Peter's very human question, "What shall we have therefore?" Did Peter learn the lesson Christ was trying to teach? The answer is given in the Book of Acts. There, we do not find Peter asking, "What will I get?" Instead we find him saying, "Such as I have give I thee"(3:6). It is a long way from "What will I get?" to "I will give what I have." Some of us may still need to make the journey.

Have You Met Yourself in This Parable?

1. Are you available to serve the Lord?

2. Are you willing to serve without a contract?

3. If nobody has hired you yet, are you willing to volunteer?

4. How did you react to the way the master paid the salaries? Did you think his system was unfair?

5. Do you ever examine your own motives as you serve the Lord?

6. Do you trust God's Word and really believe that He is generous? Or are you bitter because somebody else got what you may think is a better deal?

7. Are you a people-watcher?

Luke 19:11–27

[11]And as they heard these things, He added and spake a parable, because He was nigh to Jerusalem, and because they thought that the kingdom of God should immediately appear. [12]He said therefore, "A certain nobleman went into a far country to receive for himself a kingdom, and to return. [13]And he called his ten servants, and delivered them ten pounds, and said unto them, 'Occupy till I come.' [14]But his citizens hated him, and sent a message after him, saying, 'We will not have this man to reign over us.' [15]And it came to pass, that when he was returned, having received the kingdom, then he commanded these servants to be called unto him, to whom he had given the money, that he might know how much every man had gained by trading. [16]Then came the first, saying, 'Lord, thy pound hath gained ten pounds.' [17]And he said unto him, 'Well, thou good servant: because thou hast been faithful in a very little, have thou authority over ten cities.' [18]And the second came, saying, 'Lord, thy pound hath gained five pounds.' [19]And he said likewise to him, 'Be thou also over five cities.' [20]And another came, saying, 'Lord, behold, here is thy pound, which I have kept laid up in a napkin: [21]for I feared thee, because thou art an austere man: thou takest up that thou layedst not down, and reapest that thou didst not sow.' [22]And he saith unto him, 'Out of thine own mouth will I judge thee, thou wicked servant. Thou knewest that I was an austere man, taking up that I laid not down, and reaping that I did not sow: [23]wherefore then gavest not thou my money into the bank, that at my coming I might have required mine own with usury?' [24]And he said unto them that stood by, 'Take from him the pound, and give it to him that hath ten pounds.' [25] (And they said unto him, 'Lord, he hath ten pounds.') [26]For I say unto you, That unto every one which hath shall be given; and from him that hath not, even that he hath shall be taken away from him. [27]But those mine enemies, which would not that I should reign over them, bring hither, and slay them before Me."

13
What Happens When the King Returns?
The Parable of the Pounds

As Jesus and His followers neared Jerusalem, rumors began to circulate. "He plans to overthrow Rome!" "He will establish the throne of King David!" "The kingdom of God is here!" The unruly mobs of Passover pilgrims felt very patriotic for, after all, Passover was the commemoration of Israel's liberation from Egypt. Perhaps this Passover the nation would be liberated from Rome!

It was to silence these dangerous ideas that the Lord gave this parable. He would one day establish His kingdom, but He would first have to go away. The story He told about the nobleman was really not new to the Jewish people, for they had seen this same plot enacted years before by one of the sons of Herod the Great, Herod Archelaus (Matt. 2:22). Herod the Great left part of his kingdom to Archelaus, but the will had to be ratified by Rome. The people hated Archelaus because, though he had promised to be kinder to them than his father, he had turned out to be just as wicked. A delegation of Jewish leaders actually went to Rome to protest the approval, but Augustus ratified the appointment and Archelaus became tetrarch of Judea and Samaria. When the new ruler arrived home, he rewarded his faithful aids and punished those citizens who had opposed him.

Of course, Jesus did not tell this story for political purposes, nor should we think that our Lord is anything like that wicked ruler: Jesus used the familiar to teach the unfamiliar. Christ is the nobleman. He did not acquire His kingdom by force or guile—it was His because He is the Son of David and the Son of God. Having finished His work on earth, He went back to heaven to receive His kingdom. One day He shall return to establish that kingdom and rule as King of kings.

You and I are living in the time period between His ascension and return, and He has given us a job to do. We do not know when He shall return, but we know that when He does He will deal with the three kinds of persons found in this parable: the faithful servants, the unfaithful servant, and the rebellious citizens.

The Faithful Servants (19:15–19)
This parable is about service, not salvation. We know three facts about the faithful servants.

1. They knew their responsibility. "Do business until I come," was the nobleman's commandment. Each servant had the same amount of money and was supposed to put it to work to gain more. We must not confuse this parable with the parable of the talents (Matt. 25:14–30), though both parables deal with faithfulness. In the parable of the talents, only three servants were involved, and each was given a different amount depending on individual ability. The talents represent opportunities for them to use their abilities. In this parable there are 10 servants and each receives the same amount. The word "pound" refers to an amount of money, estimated to be worth about $20 in American money.

This raises the question about what the pound

represents. Since all the servants had the same amount, the pound must represent something that all of God's servants possess, and that can only be the Gospel message. You and I have been "put in trust with the Gospel" (1 Thes. 2:4). Paul often referred to this "stewardship of the Gospel" in his letters (1 Tim. 1:11 and 18, and 6:20; 2 Tim. 2:2). Before He returned to heaven, Jesus commissioned His follow-ers to take the Gospel to the whole world and multiply it everywhere. "Do business until I come!"

The Gospel is indeed a treasure. Paul described it as a "treasure in earthen vessels" (2 Cor. 4:7). We must guard it, but we must also invest it so that it will multiply and save many. Each believer individually, and the church collectively, has the great responsibil-ity of "doing business" with the Gospel. Everything else that we do is secondary to the great task of world evangelization.

2. *They did their job faithfully*. While we are not given the exact number of the servants who were faithful to their master, we assume that 9 out of 10 were in that category. Each took his piece of money and went out to "do business" and multiply it. As you read this parable, you can think of several excuses these men might have given for not being faithful.

"This is not a great sum of money," one of them could have argued. "Why worry about trying to put it to work?" Perhaps he was ashamed to go to the bank with such a small amount. We must never think that the message of the Gospel is something small and insignificant. Paul declared, "I am not ashamed of the Gospel of Christ: for it is the power of God unto salvation to everyone that believeth" (Rom. 1:16).

"Why bother to do business?" another could have said. "What will *I* get out of it?" The nobleman did not promise his servants anything. He simply told them to get busy. Jesus, however, has given us many promises that ought to encourage us to be faithful until He comes. And we know how this story ends: these faithful servants *were* rewarded in a munificent way. We ought to be faithful simply because Christ has commanded us, but the promised rewards do encourage us.

"How do I know he will ever come back?" is another possible excuse for doing nothing. "Our master might not make it to Rome or, if he does make the trip successfully, he might not make it back home," the servants might have reasoned. And "Furthermore, how do we know that Caesar will even grant him the kingdom? We could then find ourselves unemployed!"

Christians *know* that Jesus is coming again, that He is the King. We have no excuse for neglecting our responsibility to multiply the Gospel in this needy world. Jesus came the first time just as the Scriptures promised, and He will come the second time just as He promised He would do.

God can find others to get the job done, but if you and I fail, we lose the blessing (see Es. 4:14). There is an old story about a king who commanded six of his subjects each to bring him a bucket of fresh milk. Each of the subjects said to himself, "I'll bring a bucket of water, and nobody will know the difference." When the king dipped out of his milk, lo, it was all water! And all six farmers ended up in prison for disobeying their king.

If these men had reasons to be faithful, you and I have even more. Yet, how prone we are to make excuses. The "Gospel pound" has been in the world for nearly 20 centuries, and still there are multitudes who have never had an opportunity to hear the message of salvation.

3. They were rewarded for their faithfulness.
Remember, no reward had been promised; the gifts
given the servants were from the master's generous
heart. God does not have to reward us for serving
Him faithfully. We *ought* to be faithful. When we
consider all that He has done for us, we should be
glad to serve Him just to show our appreciation. Yet
God in His grace gives us rewards.

Please note that not all of the servants had the same
success. One man multiplied his pound 10 times,
while another multiplied his 5 times. We must not
expect everyone to produce the same results. In the
parable of the sower (Matt. 13:23), some people
produced fruit thirtyfold, some sixtyfold, and some a
hundredfold. God gives each of us different abilities
and opportunities. He does not ask us to produce the
same results, but He does ask all of us to be faithful
and do our best.

Many people have the idea that the reward for
faithfulness is less work and less responsibility, but
just the opposite is true. Imagine ruling over five
cities! Jesus taught in this parable that the reward for
faithful work is more work *and* an increased capacity
to serve the Lord. The work we do today is preparation for the work He has planned for us tomorrow.
Faithfulness is the secret of growth. If we faithfully
use the "little" that He gives us (v. 17), He will give
us more.

How do these "cities" apply to Christians today?
First, *here in this life* we have a greater capacity for
ministry and greater opportunities for service. The
pound was taken from the unfaithful servant and
given to the man with 10 pounds (vv. 24–26). What
we do not use, we may lose, and what we use
faithfully proves that we can be trusted with more.

David was faithful to take care of his father's sheep,

so God was able to entrust the nation to his care. Joshua was faithful as Moses' servant and God made him Moses' successor. Young Timothy assisted Paul in his ministry and in a few years was called to take Paul's place in the churches. Faithfulness in service indicates we are trustworthy to become rulers with God.

When Jesus comes again, He will reckon with His servants to see how faithful they have been. He will reward the faithful ones with responsibilities *in the eternal kingdom.* We do not know all that is involved in our future service for the Lord, either during His kingdom or in the new heaven and new earth. But we need to be faithful so that He can trust us with work to do for His glory.

The Unfaithful Servant (19:20–26)

Consider three facts about the unfaithful servant.

1. He knew his job but did not do it. He could not plead ignorance, for he heard the command "Do business until I come" just as did the other men. He even called the nobleman "Lord" (v. 20), yet did not do what his lord commanded. He did not lose his pound but neither did he invest it. *He saved it!* He wrapped the money in a cloth that was used for wiping perspiration from one's face, and yet he did not exert himself to produce any perspiration.

Unfaithfulness is sin. It has often been said that the greatest ability is dependability. For us to fail to do the work Christ has assigned to us is to slight His Word and insult His person. Jesus asked, "And why call ye Me, Lord, Lord, and do not the things which I say?" (Luke 6:46) Our words can never substitute for deeds.

2. He was unfaithful because his heart was not right with his master. If you had asked this servant,

"Do you believe your master is coming back?" he would have replied, "Of course I believe it!" *But he did not live what he believed.* His theology was excellent, but his practice was terrible. Many Christians today will defend the doctrine of our Lord's return but will not lift a finger to do His will.

I recently had a phone call from a fine young man who is in medical school. He and his wife sincerely want to serve Christ. "I really need to talk with you," he said, "because I want to use my training and skills in the best way to serve the Lord. I don't just want a career—I want a ministry." My friend is living in the light of the Lord's return, and because he is, I believe he will be faithful.

The servant did not love his master—he feared him. There is a proper fear of the Lord, but it is not a fear that *paralyzes* us. Rather it *mobilizes* us to serve Him. It is the reverence of a son for a father whom he dearly loves and wants to please. The Phillips version of Luke 19:21 expresses clearly the sinful attitude of this man's heart: "I have been scared—I know you're a hard man, getting something for nothing, and reaping where you never sowed."

He had no love for his master and no appreciation for what his master had done for him. If the servant had gained only one more pound, he would have become ruler of a city! This man was so afraid of life he would take no risks. He was convinced that his master was a mean selfish man who would not reward him anyway.

Love and faithfulness go together. The husband and wife who love each other will be faithful to each other. Parents who love their children will be faithful to provide for them. Christians who love their Lord will want to be faithful to Him and do the work He gives them to do. To say that our Lord is austere (v.

21) is to lie, for the word *austere* means "stern, harsh, severe." (The Greeks used this word to describe sour unripe fruit.) Jesus Christ is "meek and lowly in heart" (Matt. 11:29) and "His commandments are not grievous" (1 John 5:3).

3. *His unfaithfulness cost him his reward.* The master did not necessarily agree with the servant's words but he used them to indict the man. "If you really believed these things, then you should have worked harder!" was the master's argument. "Your words are not a reason, they are an excuse." Evangelist Billy Sunday used to define an excuse as "the skin of a reason stuffed with a lie." People who are good at excuses are rarely good at anything else.

What did the servant lose because he was unfaithful? *He lost his opportunity.* The master returned and the period of testing was over. The servant would have no further opportunities to invest the money and earn dividends. If this parable teaches us anything, it certainly teaches this: *the future is today.* What we do with *today* determines what will be done with us tomorrow.

He lost his pound. He proved unworthy of the privilege of working for the master, so his pound was given to the servant who proved he could be trusted. Verse 25 records the reaction of the people listening to Jesus: "Lord, he hath ten pounds!" In other words, "Why not give it to the man with only a few pounds?" But the biblical principle is that what we do not use we may lose, but what we gain will gain us more.

Finally, *the servant lose his reward.* The nobleman had many cities to share, but the unfaithful servant did not get one. What an indictment! This man could not be trusted with any additional work. He had not been faithful over a few things, so the master could not make him ruler over many things. "Watch yourselves, that you might not lose what we have accomplished, but that you may receive a full reward" (2 John 8, NASB). Jesus promised, "Behold, I am coming quickly, and My reward is with Me, to render to every man according to what he has done" (Rev. 22:12, NASB).

When Christ returns, He will deal with the faithful servants and the unfaithful servants, and He will also deal with a third kind of person.

The Rebellious Citizens (19:14, 27)

"We will not have this man to reign over us!" certain rebellious citizens declared. Of course, the immediate application is to the nation of Israel. Christ was near Jerusalem and many expected Him to establish His kingdom. But Jesus did not come to change Israel's politics, He came to change men's hearts. When He rode into Jerusalem, Jesus presented Himself as a humble King, not a violent conqueror. Led by the spiritually blind rulers, the nation rejected Him and said, "We have no king but Caesar!"

What were the consequences of this rebellion? In a few years, Jerusalem was reduced to shambles by the Roman armies, and the temple was destroyed. The Jewish nation was dispersed across the face of the earth to wander "many days, without a king, and without a prince" (Hosea 3:4).

But there is a much wider application. When the Lord returns, He will have to punish those who would not bow before Him and submit to His will. This world belongs to God, and the people in the world are citizens who must depend on God whether they know it or not. As the Creator-King, God gives to this world all that it needs. "He did good, and gave us rain from heaven, and fruitful seasons, filling our hearts with food and gladness" (Acts 14:17). And, "He giveth to all life, and breath, and all things. . . . For in Him we live, and move, and have our being" (Acts 17:25, 28).

It is understandable that those Jewish citizens could hate Archelaus, son of Herod the Great, because he was a cruel and selfish man. But how could anyone hate Jesus Christ? "But his citizens hated him . . . " (v. 14). Jesus had lived among them. He had taught them God's truth, healed their sick bodies, and even raised the dead. He had brought hope and comfort to their lives. Their rulers had to bribe false witnesses in order to try Him, because there could be no true indictment against the perfect Son of God.

Sad to say, most of the people in our world want nothing to do with Jesus Christ. "There is none that understandeth, there is none that seeketh after God" (Rom. 3:11). But God is seeking after men! "For the Son of man is come to seek and to save that which was lost" (Luke 19:10). Jesus made that statement just before He gave this parable.

When the Lord returns, it will mean reward for the faithful, loss of reward for the unfaithful, and terrible judgment for the unbelieving, rebellious people who rejected Him: "In flaming fire taking vengeance on them that know not God, and that obey not the Gospel of our Lord Jesus Christ. Who shall be punished with everlasting destruction from the presence of the Lord, and from the glory of His power" (2 Thes. 1:8–9).

A student stopped me after a Sunday School lesson and asked, "Do you think the heathen are lost?" My reply stunned him, "Yes, I do, and the heathen *in this city* are more lost than anybody else because they have had greater opportunities to be saved."

This is not a day of judgment, it is a day of grace,

and any rebellious citizen can be saved. The Lord "is longsuffering to usward, not willing that any should perish, but that all should come to repentance" (2 Peter 3:9). Jesus Christ died for us *when we were His enemies* (Rom. 5:10). We can conceive of a man giving his life for his friends, but certainly not for his enemies. Yet that is what Jesus did. Our very thinking was at enmity with God (Rom. 8:7), yet He loved us and gave His Son to die for us.

Augustus Caesar never did give Archaleus the title of king. But Jesus Christ is King of kings (Rev. 19:16).

A review of this parable reveals three kinds of people: the faithful servants *who do good*, the unfaithful servants *who do nothing*, and the rebellious citizens *who do evil*. Jesus Christ will deal with all of them when He returns and the judgment will be just.

Have you Met Yourself in This Parable?

1. Which group are you in: the faithful, the unfaithful, or the rebellious?

2. Have you invested the Gospel so that it is producing dividends in your life?

3. What excuses are you giving (if any) for your unfaithfulness?

4. What *new* ways of multiplying the Gospel have you come up with lately?

5. Do you live in the light of Christ's soon return?